Mainstreaming
ideas for teaching young children

Mainstreaming
ideas for teaching young children

by
Judith Souweine,
Sheila Crimmins,
and Carolyn Mazel

The Early Education Center
Amherst-Pelham Public Schools
Amherst, Massachusetts

National Association for the Education of Young Children
Washington, D.C.

Photographs: Lionel J-M Delevingne
Cover art: Rebecca J. Miller

Library of Congress Catalog Card Number: 81-83869
ISBN Catalog Number: 0-912674-77-6
NAEYC #114

Printed in the United States of America.

To the families and children of the Early Education Center

Contents

Acknowledgments

We wish to acknowledge the many people who have encouraged and guided us to the completion of this book.

For their critical reviews of the manuscript, a special note of appreciation is extended to Rosemary Agoglia, Bill Allen, Ellen Berson, Fleet Hill, Stan Kulikowski, Linda Nober, and Judith Weinthaler. Bill Ensslin deserves a special thank-you for his contributions to the language section.

We wish to thank John Burgess, our Special Education Director, for his continuing support of this project. We are grateful for Ella Mazel's editing of the manuscript.

Ken Blanchard's work has influenced both our theory and practice as we work with children, parents, and each other.

We are most indebted to the children and parents of the Early Education Center who have taught us and inspired our growth and learning.

Introduction

The movement to mainstream special needs children in the least restrictive environments, coupled with the emphasis on early identification of and intervention for these children, has led to increasing numbers of integrated early childhood programs. This book is based on experiences providing services to children with special needs in a setting with regular needs students (children without special needs). Our previous experiences with nonintegrated special education programs, as well as our belief in the values of integration, provided the framework for our endeavors. Our initial excitement was replaced by the growing pains of program development. Continual self-evaluation, responses from parents, and integration of new knowledge and theory has provided the basis for an everchanging, evolving program. Growing pains have been replaced by feelings of staff competence and openness to new ideas. Working together as a team of staff and parents, we have developed assessment strategies, a curriculum, and evaluation procedures that have enabled us to deliver comprehensive services to children. Each year new families provide us with different challenges; working through the dynamics of a professional team is an ongoing process.

The process of bringing together special and regular needs young children enriches the lives of both. We anticipate that the program recommendations offered throughout this book will be helpful to others who work with young children in a variety of situations. Although funding levels, staffing patterns, facilities, and program philosophies will differ, the general principles of child growth, development, and learning remain the same for all children.

The Amherst Program

The Early Education Center (EEC) of the Amherst-Pelham Public Schools, Amherst, Massachusetts, is an integrated program serving 15 children, ages three to five, about one-half of whom have special needs. The program was developed in response to the Massachusetts Special Education Law Chapter 766, and the federal government's P.L. 94-142, which require school systems to serve special needs children beginning at age three.

The special needs children in the group range in severity of handicap.

The class has always included children who were delayed in many areas (e.g., no language, inability to walk, not toilet trained) as well as children with a difficulty in only one area (e.g., language, emotional development, visual impairment). Regular needs children live in the community; because there are more children who wish to attend than there are spaces, the names are drawn at random. The regular needs students pay tuition to attend the program, while those who have special needs receive services at no charge to their parents. Funding for the program is provided by the town as well as by P.L. 94-142 entitlement funds.

The staff of the EEC includes an early childhood special education teacher, an aide, a part-time speech and language therapist, and a part-time preschool coordinator. Children with special needs receive a variety of services in the program, based on their individual requirements. They each attend a half-day nursery program, and their parents are involved in various advisory and instructional roles (see Chapter 5). In addition, speech and language therapy is provided in the classroom. Other services such as physical therapy, psychological therapy, or audiological services, are arranged by contract with professionals in the community.

Rationale

This book describes the philosophy, approach, strategies, and sample activities used by the staff of the Early Education Center to successfully integrate special needs students into a regular nursery classroom. The challenge has been to meet the developmental needs of both groups of children without sacrificing the needs of either.

The rationale underlying the program is threefold:

1. Special needs children will learn to function best in the educational mainstream if they are placed in integrated facilities.

2. Special needs children will increase in their skill development by observation and interaction with regular needs children.

3. All the children will become more sensitive to individual differences by developing early relationships with special needs children.

Merely placing handicapped students into regular environments will not accomplish the goals of increased skill development or sensitivity. As Guralnick (1976) states, "The critical component is not the simple presence of non-handicapped children in the class but the way in which interactions among these children are *systematically* guided and encouraged" (p. 236). In this book we present strategies for integrating young children derived from our experiences with a wide range of handicapped children who were grouped with regular needs age-mates.

In the first chapter we outline the major questions the staff of the EEC has dealt with in formulating and refining the program to integrate special needs students into regular needs classrooms. It is our hope that the resolution of these questions can provide a framework for other practitioners. In Chapter 2 we describe the process of developing the individualized educational plan (IEP) for each child and methods for measuring progress toward the goals and objectives of the plan. In Chapter 3 we describe the physical environment of the classroom, with particular attention to how the different areas enhance the integration process and coincide with the children's varying developmental levels. In order to convey the integration process itself, we present in Chapter 4 the structure of the day organized by activity periods, with sample activities for each period. All aspects of the day are designed to provide opportunities to meet the general and specific objectives for the children. The sample activities in this chapter are not meant to provide a comprehensive curriculum for an entire year; there are numerous activity and curriculum books available for teachers to use in devising a curriculum appropriate for the children with whom they work. (See Croft and Hess 1975; Forman and Hill 1980; Hohmann, Banet, and Weikart 1979.) Rather, this book provides examples of how regular early childhood activities can be modified to include children at varying levels of functioning. In the final chapter we detail the EEC's strategies for involving parents in the education of their children. Professional books and articles, parenting materials, and children's books are listed in the Bibliography.

When we began the process of program development, we had a theoretical and philosophical commitment to mainstreaming. We did not, however, have specific training as to how to do it. We hope that these chapters provide examples and information that will enable others with a similar commitment to young children to develop successful programs as well.

1 | Questions about Mainstreaming

Research (Allen, Benning, and Drummond 1972; Guralnick 1976) and experience suggest that a regular early childhood program cannot merely enroll some handicapped children (or vice versa) and let things happen; rather, careful planning for parents, teachers, and children is essential.

Integrating special needs and regular needs children in an early childhood program raises many questions and fears for parents, children, and staff. Some of the questions relate to program planning; that is, how the teacher is going to make the program work. Other questions relate to parent concerns; parents worry about the effects of the program on their own children's development. These concerns require clear answers based on research and experiences. The children themselves also raise important questions that necessitate creative teacher responses.

In this chapter, the most common *questions* pertaining to integrating special needs and nonspecial needs young children are presented. We explain the Early Education Center's *approaches* to resolving various issues, and offer real-life *examples* so that others might implement these successful strategies.

Question: How can teachers structure activities so that children with varying abilities can participate?

Approach: In planning all activities for young children, thought must be given to how an activity can be flexible enough to accommodate different levels of participation in a particular skill area. As often as possible the process of the activity (cooking, pasting, block building) will take precedence over any resulting product. Each child will feel more comfortable being involved if the emphasis is on the enjoyment of doing rather than on the completion of a product. The teacher's responsibility is to ensure every child feels some success in the experience by providing the appropriate balance of direction, support, and independence each child needs to participate at an optimal level.

Example: The children are making Valentine cards. Karen is a very

1

In planning all activities for young children, thought must be given to how an activity can be flexible enough to accommodate different levels of participation in a particular skill area.

competent child who can cut, glue, write some letters, and create imaginative projects. John is a younger child who has severe developmental delays. A teacher needs to be with him, guiding him through a simple task, seeing that he stays with it for five minutes. Stephen can glue but has difficulty cutting.

To make the activity successful for each of these children, the teacher provides a range of materials: hearts drawn on sheets of paper, hearts already cut from paper and fabric, heart stickers that are to be peeled off a backing sheet and stuck on paper, scissors, glue, yarn, construction paper, and crayons.

John can decorate his paper with heart stickers, using his fine motor control skills, while not needing cutting or pasting skills. He might also be helped to color his card. Stephen, who glues but is not yet ready to cut, has access to several precut materials, which he can paste in different ways on his card. Karen can be urged to cut out predrawn shapes, draw and cut her own shapes, paste, and write a message on her card. All the children have access to the same materials. They are free to select those they are able to use and are guided by the teacher in finding within the same activity an individual project that is challenging yet guarantees success. There is no model Valentine for children to copy.

Question: How can all the children be encouraged to function at their optimal level rather than a regressed or immature one?

Approach: Regardless of ability, children can be praised for what they are able to do. The teacher thus helps each child feel successful.

Example: While the children are making Valentine cards, the teacher can praise each child as the activity progresses. "Karen, it looks like you're cutting all the curves in the heart very carefully." "Stephen, you're finding lots of different ways to stick the hearts on your card." "John, you're doing a fine job sitting at the table with Karen and Stephen making your Valentine." The teacher helps all of the children feel successful by being aware of what they are doing and commenting to them about it.

Question: How can teachers help alleviate the fears of the parents of regular needs children that their children will learn inappropriate behavior exhibited by special needs children?

Approach: Cooke's research (Cooke et al. 1977) and our experience indicate that regular needs children will not imitate special needs children's inappropriate behavior unless it is directly reinforced by teachers or peers. Therefore, the teacher must monitor and analyze any reinforcement that emerges in response to inappropriate behavior. Behavior of children that is indicative of delay or regression is usually easier to deal with than acting out behavior because the latter is often reinforced by peers rather than adults. Imitation of delayed behavior is often not functional for the regular needs child and therefore soon disappears, but teachers should be prepared for children who try out unfamiliar behaviors.

The teacher can explain this to concerned parents, but the best response is often to have the parent talk to other parents whose children have been in mainstreamed classrooms. The following examples are typical of situations parents might observe.

Example: Seth is unable to reproduce many speech sounds correctly. Maria starts imitating his speech. The teacher can choose to ignore these imitations, thus removing any extra attention to Maria. Another strategy might include telling Maria that it is difficult to understand what she says when she talks like Seth. The teacher can explain that Seth is learning to speak correctly and until he does the teachers and children can help him by trying hard to understand him.

Example of maladaptive behavior: Adam displays many behaviors that disrupt the class and have the effect of making the children laugh, thereby providing peer reinforcement to Adam. Eddie wants to be liked by Adam and also would like to have the children's attention focused on him. It is necessary for the teacher to find ways to limit the other children's attention to both Adam and Eddie. One of the easiest ways is to remove Adam for a brief time from the activity so that he cannot receive the children's attention. At the same time the teacher should praise the children who are participating appropriately. The teacher should *not* give additional attention to Adam for his disruptive behavior. When he returns to the activity the teacher can say, "I'm glad to see you back with us, and I see you are trying hard to follow the rules." It is important for the teacher to be aware of both Adam and Eddie's needs for attention and approval and ensure that they receive more attention for appropriate rather than inappropriate behavior.

Question: How can teachers prepare a group of children for entry of a severely impaired child?

Approach: Explain the disability in an easy-to-understand way; use books (see Bibliography), pictures, and films to make it more concrete; talk about the children's expectations and fears.

Example: Paul wears braces on his legs and has severe cognitive and emotional delays. The fact that Paul wears braces is likely to be more salient and frightening to the children than the fact that he functions about two or three years below his age level in some areas. In order to prepare the children for Paul, the teacher finds picture books on handicaps; one about a boy whose legs are like Paul's, another about a man with an artificial limb. After reading the story to the class, the teacher asks questions like, "What do you think it would feel like to walk like the boy in the story?" The teacher tells the class about Paul's upcoming entry, emphasizing the things he can do, while mentioning things with which he will have trouble. Teachers should not be surprised if children do not have many questions or comments initially. Until the children see Paul, the idea of braces is not very concrete. After he comes to school, the class is likely to have many questions, and the teachers must be open to them as they arise.

Later in the year teachers can bring in old braces and crutches for the children to try. They see for themselves how difficult it is to sit and stand with leg braces, and can develop a better understanding of what Paul experiences.

Question: What can teachers do when children ask about or ridicule another child's disability?

Approach: Confirm the child's perception of the disability and then give a frank explanation of it.

Example: The children have arrived at school and are participating in morning circle. Each child has an opportunity to make an announcement. Sandy is a special needs child with a severe speech problem; many times her utterances are completely unintelligible. This morning at circle she makes an announcement that no one understands. The teacher asks her to repeat it, but after two repetitions it is still not clear. The teacher thanks Sandy for sharing her announcement. Jonathan asks, "What did she say?" "I don't know what she said, Jonathan," the teacher replies.

The teacher has responded to Jonathan honestly, showing him she shares his inability to understand Sandy. The teacher then goes on to explain that Sandy has a hard time saying certain words, and that she is working with the speech therapist who will teach her to speak better. This might be followed by a statement about other children in the class needing help to speak more clearly too.

Teachers should provide activities which bring special needs and regular needs children in contact with each other but should not be alarmed if all children do not choose to play with some of the special needs children.

Situations like this arise frequently in an integrated setting. Paul is a special needs child who wears leg braces. When Samuel first sees Paul he laughs and is asked for a reason. "He walks funny." This opens a discussion of why it seems funny and why Paul needs braces. The teacher explains that before Paul had leg braces he was in a wheelchair. Now he wears braces because he is learning to walk.

Question: How can teachers help children who are frightened by another child's disability?

Approach: These children are probably afraid that a similar problem will affect their own bodies. Explain in an understandable way how the child was born or became disabled. Allow the children to carefully explore the disabled child's prosthesis, stroller, wheelchair, or braces. This helps to remove some of the stigma and mystery attached to them. Encourage questions and answer them as honestly and directly as possible.

Example: The teacher had prepared the class for a new child who could neither walk nor talk. Yet when Louis, who has cerebral palsy, first entered the class both Linda and Mary burst into tears. They said they were scared because Louis made loud noises. Mary later went home and told her parents, "Louis was like that because of a car accident" (her own explanation of why Louis could not walk). She also told her mother she would not return to school. Her parents and the teacher worked out a plan for her to return to school the next day; she was told she could leave after one hour. The teacher tried to help Mary understand that Louis had some characteristics like her own; how he could do some of the things she could. It was essential to Mary and Louis's success in the class that she come to school the next day. She had no interest in leaving after an hour and stayed happily through the morning.

All of the children needed time to adjust to Louis; some adjusted faster than others. After two weeks most of the questions about Louis were resolved and the children were happy to learn all the things Louis *could* do. They had tried out his stroller and corrective shoes. Exploration with the symbols of his handicap helped to discharge some fear. When Louis waved at the class, one four-year-old child evidenced both his caring and confusion about Louis by saying, "Hey, he waves like a human being."

Question: How can teachers encourage appreciation and acceptance of special needs children by regular needs children?

Approach: One of the crucial premises that the EEC staff operates from is that all the children are more alike than they are different. Everyone is appreciated for their personality in a nonevaluative manner. This attitude provides an atmosphere of acceptance that encourages mutual appreciation rather than of competition.

Example: The teacher says, "Good, John, you're doing the motions of 'She'll Be Coming 'Round the Mountain.'" A few days later Karen notices that John is imitating the gestures in another song. She comments to the teacher, "John is making the signs!" The teacher can then help Karen direct her excitement to John by saying, "You sound pretty excited about that, Karen. Why don't you tell John?" This way the responsibility for encouraging participation becomes shared. The regular needs child is then praised by the teacher for helping John feel good about his performance.

Question: When and how should teachers intervene in problem social situations between special needs children and regular needs children?

Approach: Both special and regular needs children will require teacher help in problem situations. The regular needs child will be assisted by teacher help in talking with or interpreting the special needs child. The special needs child will need guidance in responding appropriately to requests and directions from age-mates.

Example: Karen has made an elaborate structure with the large blocks which she is calling her house. John suddenly plops himself in the middle of it, disturbing her play. She asks him to leave and he ignores her request. The teachers know that John is unable to respond to such a request because he does not respond to verbal directions, and he will continue to ignore any further overtures. The teacher intervenes, knowing that the children's interaction is at a standstill. Karen is praised immediately for asking John to leave in a nice way. The teacher then repeats Karen's request to John and physically leads him away to another activity. When the social and play skills of the children differ to such a degree, it is often the role of the teacher to guide the children through a social interchange they could not complete on their own. The teacher's intervention is designed to reinforce Karen's use of verbal problem solving, prevent Karen from becoming frustrated with and angry at John, and provide John with a model social interchange.

Question: When the pace of the children differs, how do teachers structure transitions in the daily routine?

Approach: Teachers must plan specific interventions for specific children during transitions. A consistent schedule helps all the children anticipate and prepare for activity changes.

Example: Two beeps on the horn signified to the children it was time to clean up. Karen immediately yells, "Clean-up time," interrupts her play, and starts to put away the toys. Prior to the beeps, a teacher has taken John by the hand. After the sound, she repeats, "It's time to clean up and you may put these blocks away." This specific direction removes an opportunity for John to run away and disrupt clean-up time. John needs teacher intervention to slow him down.

A second example of pace differences occurs with Jason, who moves more slowly than the other children. Anticipating the transition time enables the teacher to get him started early. An objective for Jason is to get him to move more quickly. Delaying tactics such as asking lots of questions are ignored and fast movements are praised. It is necessary to make it clear to Jason that if he moves slowly to the next activity he will miss part of it and/or will be left behind by the other children.

Question: What can teachers do when regular needs children express suspicion of or disgust for a special needs child?

Approach: This is likely to arise with special needs children who look different. The teacher models tolerance and acceptance for regular needs children, demonstrating the importance of understanding differences among people.

Example: Some children do not like sitting next to Paul because he leans on them for balance and drools. While some shy away from him without saying anything, others state that they do not like sitting with Paul because he drools.

This is a difficult problem that we have not yet resolved satisfactorily. If children choose to sit next to Paul and then change their mind because of the drooling, they are asked to stick to their original choice of sitting next to Paul. When the question was discussed with the group, we found that some children who were more accepting of Paul from the start displayed their acceptance even more openly afterward. These children were then praised for their behavior.

In Paul's case, the disturbing behavior is one that can be controlled, so the children can be asked to remind Paul to swallow and praise him for doing so. Other disabilities are not controllable, such as his spasticity, and in these cases the regular needs children learn that people are

Our staff has always attempted to pair the most difficult child with the most experienced staff member.

different and cannot always change.

Most adults have experienced unease at the sight of severely disabled people. It sometimes takes a conscious reminder that they are still people who happen to look different and have some different as well as many similar needs. Children in an integrated program must be permitted to adjust gradually. Some children may not be any less suspicious by the end of the year, but many will be very open and accepting. By structuring the class in a way that involves all the children in comfortable, positive interactions, it is hoped that the regular needs children will at least see that everyone is a valued group member.

Question: What can teachers do to ensure that all the children interact with each other?

Approach: Teachers should provide activities that bring special needs and regular needs children in contact with each other, but should not be alarmed if all children do not choose to play with some of the special needs children. Specific activities may need to be structured to encourage interaction between some children.

Example: Eddie, a child with severe developmental delays, is cooking one morning with three other children and a teacher. One child, Patty, has mild speech problems, and José and Jean are regular needs students. During the activity, the teacher encourages the children to help each other. José helps Eddie measure a cup of flour and is praised by the teacher for this. José seems to enjoy being able to help Eddie with the cooking tasks. When they finish it is time for free play. José becomes involved in dramatic play with Jean and Patty while Eddie plays at the water table.

Since Eddie is not at José's level of imaginative play, it does not seem reasonable for the teacher to intervene and force the interaction in free play. José is likely to play for a few minutes at the water table where give and take between special and regular needs children can be encouraged. Because there are such differences in skill levels, the teacher structures the day so that some activities will bring children together, and others will allow them to develop their own play at their own levels of ability.

Question: How does a teacher integrate a severely behavior-disordered child into the class?

Approach: The manifestations of a behavior disorder are many, but most of the children in our experience seem to be one of two types: those who are negative and aggressive, and therefore act out; and those who have limited skills and are thus disruptive to the class. The first type of children are oppositional, angry, and avoid adult demands. They are often very bright. Limited skills children are often bizarre, hyperactive, and avoid adult contact. In order to integrate these children the teacher will need extra support: an adult to act as the children's controls while they experience the new situation. Strategies for dealing with behavior-disordered children follow in two sections.

Acting out child. One adult is assigned to be with the acting out child at all times when the child first enters the program. Any impulse to act out, such as to throw a chair or hit a child, is stopped by the adult. The adult confirms the rule for the child, "no throwing/no hurting," and firmly tells the child that teachers will not allow children to hurt anyone in the class, and then states the consequence for breaking the rule. The child feels protected by the adult's control and the consistency of knowing the rules and the consequences for breaking the rules. At the same time, the teacher is playing with the child to decide the theme and style of the play. This allows the child to make choices and exert control where it is appropriate. It is important for the teacher to have planned how to handle the series of control battles or power struggles that will occur when integrating an aggressive child, and to have decided consequences in advance. It might be helpful to make a list of all the things a child may do, for example, hit, spit, swear, throw chairs, etc., and decide which behaviors will be ignored and which will be followed by imposition of a consequence. These are personal choices; for example, some teachers tolerate swearing while others do not. It is essential for the teacher to maintain self-control and act from a plan rather than succumb to the anger these children are very adept at provoking in adults. Table 1 is an example of a teacher's plan.

Example: Peter was a four-year-old boy referred to us by his mother who said she was at the end of her rope with him. She reported she had always had a difficult time controlling him and making him happy even when he was a baby. He was physically and verbally abusive to adults and children. His mother decided to seek help when during the previous week he took her car keys and started the engine of her new car, and moved from lighting cigarettes to lighting a fire in their basement. Peter had already been requested to leave his previous nursery school.

During screening, Peter told the examiner to "shut-up or he'd put her

Table 1.
Teacher plan for handling negative behavior

Negative behavior	Consequences
hurting, throwing, hitting, kicking	Remove children from play, remind them of rule about no hurting, and have children sit isolated in chair for two minutes. Then have children state the rule. Children can then return to play.
tantrums	Remove children to area where their tantrum will not interfere with others. Ignore behavior. Restrain if necessary using minimum physical contact. Talk to children when their tantrum is over, but saving face is important for all children. They may refuse to talk about what happened because of embarrassment. Teachers must respect this.
swearing	Ignore swearing if possible; acting out children need some way to express their anger; this may be a big step for them to move from being physically abusive to verbally abusive. Develop a strategy that allows you to stay calm.
spitting	Ask peers to tell spitting children they do not want to be spit at. Remind children that people have asked them not to spit and that if they forget the teacher will have to intervene and the spitting children will have to leave play.
fighting over toys	Help children develop skills for working out their problems without teacher intervention. Ask them to say, "May I have a turn?" and if refused to ask, "When will you be finished?"

face on the ceiling." After he had been evaluated and placed in the EEC program, the head teacher was assigned to stay with him all morning during his first few days at school. When he arrived, the teacher explained to him there were two rules: no hurting and no throwing. She said she would help him to remember them. Peter was happy to see all the toys and because he was bright and imaginative he played well with the adventure toys (small figures and accompanying planes, boats, tents). The teacher followed Peter's game and played the way he wanted. This encouraged him to feel safe with this adult and he began to let down his guard. When he did break either rule the teacher very firmly said, "No hurting, you will have to leave the game." Often at this point Peter would have a tantrum and scream abuses. The teacher picked him up and put him in the time out chair. He sat there (sometimes having to be held in the chair) until he was quiet for two minutes. When the two minutes were up, the teacher asked, "What is the rule?" Peter was expected to say "no hurting." The teacher had to model this at first. It was important with Peter to keep this exchange as short as possible. Otherwise he got the "ho-hum, I've heard all this before look" on his face that meant he was beyond listening.

At the same time Peter's negative behavior was monitored very closely, the teacher structured lots of successes for Peter and praised him. He began to respond to praise and seek it out rather than just trying to get attention for being oppositional. The teacher also worked closely with his mother who followed through with many of the same consequences for negative behavior at home. Peter's old patterns began to be useless and he was able to change to positive patterns. After two months he no longer hurt people; he occasionally would get angry and swear at people but he would usually mutter to himself and leave the situation voluntarily.

Disruptive child. Children with limited skills also require a great deal of planning. These children are not actively aggressive but rather avoid other people and stimulation. They often make bizarre movements and noises and their behavior is generally erratic. The other children in the class are likely to describe these children as babies. It is the easiest way for them to understand children who do not play and do not understand the rules and the teachers. Because these children's influence is usually disruptive, they are often scapegoated.

It is important to move slowly with these children. First, help them become accustomed to the room without the added stimulation of the other children and their activity. Gradually have each child come to class during the time that erratic behavior would appear least disruptive. Begin expecting these children to respond to the one most familiar adult assigned to be with them. Avoid letting them disrupt other children's games and play so they do not immediately react negatively to the new child. Manually guide disruptive children to do what is expected of the others and praise them for doing so even if they do not appear to care. Young children's learning rates can be erratic. The more consistent the teacher is the more likely their rate of learning will increase.

In many groups a child with limited skills is assigned to an aide who frequently is less experienced than the head teacher. Our staff has always attempted to pair the most difficult child with the most experienced staff member.

Example: Alison was referred to the program by her parents because she was extremely hyperactive, echolalic, and unmanageable at home. After the evaluation process was completed on her third birthday, she was enrolled. Since she had never been in a school or play group, we did not know how she was going to respond to the classroom situation. We predicted separation difficulties, which did occur. She was initially scheduled for a short time one morning, accompanied by her mother; she refused to leave her mother's arms. In the following days we attempted brief separations from the mother that resulted in prolonged screaming. Because it is rare that anyone other than the disabled child's parents have cared for them, it is often a difficult and slow process to transfer the child to another adult. At this point we chose to change our strategy and have her come to school in the afternoon when no other children were there. This would enable the teacher to give her full attention to Alison, and her screaming would not be disruptive to the other students. We were also concerned that the other children would form very negative impressions of her if the screaming continued. The change in plans was difficult for Alison's parents; they were anxious to have her go to school like the other children. We could not predict how long it would take Alison to be reintroduced to the morning session. We made a plan with her parents detailing the following conditions: Alison would come to school for an hour a day in the afternoon. Her crying would be monitored and graphed; when the crying was reduced to 15 minutes she could begin in the morning. For two weeks Alison came to school in the afternoon. In the next two weeks she came in the morning for a shortened day. She gradually worked up to a two-and-one-half-hour day that was still shorter than the other students'. She came during times that she could be successful and when the teacher could be available to her. This meant missing the morning circle and part of the activity period because the sitting and listening required was much too difficult for her. When she was present for the activity period it was necessary to plan a simple task that she could do with adult direction. Throughout the day Alison required extra supervision and monitoring. Her limited skills made task completion, making choices, cleaning up, and playing with toys difficult. The teacher needed to manually guide and prompt her through these tasks and their component parts and praise Alison for her successes.

2 | Developing the Individualized Educational Plan

P.L. 94-142 mandates a series of steps that must be taken before a special needs child can receive services. These steps, including the development of the individualized educational plan (IEP), are described in this chapter. The IEP provides the structure for delivering services for each child based on assessment of the child's needs.

Identifying young children with special needs

In order to identify and serve young children with special needs, school systems are required to
1. publicize the availability of services,
2. screen children to find those who may need further evaluation,
3. assess those who are thought to be in need of special services,
4. devise an IEP for those in need,
5. deliver the services needed, and
6. evaluate the progress of the children served.

P.L. 94-142 requires that these steps be taken for children between the ages of 6 and 21 who have special educational needs. Similar services for children birth to 6 years old are permissible under federal law if states so choose.

Steps 1 and 2 are outlined in Meisels (1979a) and will not be discussed further here. The third step, assessment, must be designed to provide information about the child's strengths and weaknesses upon which the IEP can be developed.

Issues and assumptions in assessing young children

A comprehensive assessment involves the collection and synthesis of information from those who are familiar with the child as well as the seeking of new information. The purposes of assessment are (1) to identify the child's strengths and weaknesses, (2) to determine the nature and cause of problems or deficiencies, and (3) to make recom-

Parents can effectively be involved in the assessment process by asking them what questions they would like answered about their child. The needs identified by the team are grouped into some general focus areas and parent and teacher priorities are established.

mendations for suitable remediation.

The assessment of young children differs markedly from the assessment of older children for several reasons. Young children develop at a more rapid pace than older children, and they are often unpredictable or uncooperative during assessment procedures. The tests administered must be designed for young children, and should be validated for the population with whom they are used. Because young children are often not enrolled in school, locating them may require intensive community efforts.

Assessment procedures for young children must be designed to minimize these differences. Those who assess young children should be well trained and experienced in child development in order to recognize behaviors that fall into the wide range of normal. Experienced early childhood professionals will use a variety of skills to establish rapport with the young child, thereby increasing the possibility that the child's performance will be the best possible. Because a child's performance at any session may be influenced by factors such as fear, fatigue, shyness, or recent events, several assessment sessions are recommended.

In addition to formal assessments, information must be solicited from parents about their children's history and current pattern of abilities and difficulties. Contact with parents also provides information about children's ethnic, linguistic, and socioeconomic backgrounds. Valid assessments must take all these factors into account in determining and defining the children's level of competence.

Because young children exhibit different levels of ability depending on the setting and circumstances, assessment should include observation in a variety of settings. Assessments made in homes and classrooms are often the most reliable. Standardized assessment procedures for young children are not yet well developed. Thus, informal assessments contribute greatly to obtaining an accurate, comprehensive picture of the child.

Steps in the assessment process

After a child has been *screened* (see Meisels 1979a for a complete description of screening), it is determined whether the child should be referred for further assessment. Screening does not diagnose or describe a child's needs but simply indicates that a child may have special needs and may also identify some of the areas for concern. Figure 1 outlines the steps in the assessment process.

Referral. Children are referred for further assessment if the screening, classroom observations, or results of other assessments warrant it. A list of reasons for referral is provided. For example, a referral might indicate "Poor scores on the screening test in speech and language. Parents report delayed speech and difficulty understanding child."

Assign coordinator. After a child is referred, an assessment coordinator is assigned who will be responsible for facilitating communication among all people involved in the assessment and for scheduling meetings.

Coordinator meets with parents. The coordinator meets with the child's parents to gather information about the child and to inform the parents of the components of the process and their rights. Written permissions should be obtained to release their child's records and to complete the assessment. The coordinator should elicit parents' observations and concerns about their child, as well as relevant information such as any history of problems, previous evaluations, and names of other professionals and agencies who have worked with the child. Parents will undoubtedly have many questions about assessment procedures, services, and follow-up. The coordinator should be prepared to discuss these concerns and provide pamphlets, for the parents to take home, which will respond to these questions.

Parents can effectively be involved in the assessment process by asking them what questions they would like answered about their child. This initial list of questions can be augmented with questions from

Figure 1.
The assessment process

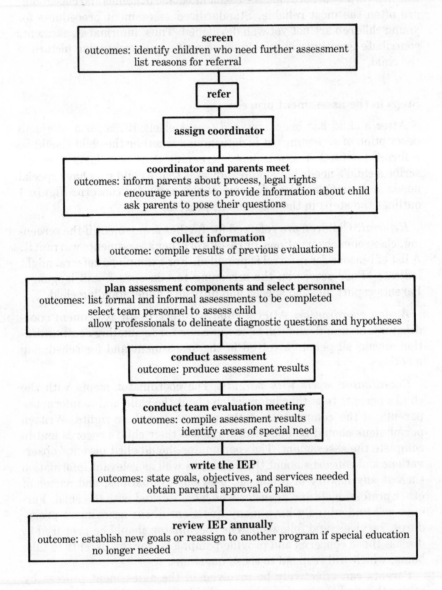

screen
outcomes: identify children who need further assessment
list reasons for referral

refer

assign coordinator

coordinator and parents meet
outcomes: inform parents about process, legal rights
encourage parents to provide information about child
ask parents to pose their questions

collect information
outcome: compile results of previous evaluations

plan assessment components and select personnel
outcomes: list formal and informal assessments to be completed
select team personnel to assess child
allow professionals to delineate diagnostic questions and hypotheses

conduct assessment
outcome: produce assessment results

conduct team evaluation meeting
outcomes: compile assessment results
identify areas of special need

write the IEP
outcomes: state goals, objectives, and services needed
obtain parental approval of plan

review IEP annually
outcome: establish new goals or reassign to another program if special education
no longer needed

others involved in the assessment. By listing their questions, parents can be more assured that their goals for the assessment will be met in addition to the goals set by the professionals. Sometimes parents ask questions that cannot be answered. The coordinator can explain which questions the assessment team will attempt to answer and which ones are beyond their expertise or cannot be predicted. Helping parents narrow their questions to answerable ones lessens the possibility that they will be disappointed or surprised in the assessment process. Parents frequently ask: "Is my child retarded?" "Why does he run around so much?" "Will my son learn to walk and when can I expect it to happen?" "Is my daughter any better behaved around other people?" Examples of questions parents might ask, but that are difficult to answer, are "Will he always be like this?" and "Is it our fault that she is this way?"

Parents must also be given a thorough explanation of their legal rights in the assessment process as required by P.L. 94-142. Parents should be aware that if their child is identified as handicapped, the child cannot be denied a free education. All children must be tested fairly, and when enrolled in a program, an IEP must be devised for the child. Special needs children must be placed in the least restrictive environment, i.e., generally with regular needs children. Programs funded through P.L. 94-142 are required to deal fairly with parents and must allow them to participate in the child's education (Turnbull 1981).

Sometimes it may be necessary to have more than one meeting with parents to cover all the diagnostic and legal issues. Coordinators must be prepared to answer many questions as there is a lot of information for parents to assimilate.

Collect information. After meeting with the parents and obtaining permission, the coordinator sends for copies of previous assessments, including teachers' reports, health examinations, and recommendations from other specialists. Professionals can respond to specific questions about the reasons for referral. For example, if a parent is concerned about the child's high activity level, medical personnel may be able to comment on any organic or nutritional problems and the teacher can describe activity levels in class.

Plan assessment components and select personnel. The child's areas needing further assessment become clearer after collecting information from parents and others. Decisions about which assessments to complete will depend on the child's disabilities as well as legal requirements. State laws specify the components of a team evaluation, but the typical areas of investigation, the personnel involved, and the information obtained are listed in table 2.

Table 2.
Components of a team evaluation

Area of investigation	Personnel involved	Information obtained
social and developmental history, home interview	social worker or guidance counselor	social and emotional history; developmental milestones; pertinent family history; effect of the child's problems on the family unit
physical examination	physician or nurse	general health; medical history; physical, sensory, or neurological problems
psychological examination	psychologist	intellectual, emotional functioning
hearing examination	audiologist	hearing ability and any impairment
speech and language evaluation	speech pathologist	quality of receptive and expressive language; articulation
educational evaluation	special education/ early childhood teacher	functioning in classroom; skills and achievement in school

Depending on the child's specific problems, additional assessments may be prepared by a physical therapist, occupational therapist, neurologist, psychiatrist, or another specialist. Information from these sources should be synthesized and used to plan the next assessment. Background information such as the family history, medical examination(s), and educational history should be obtained before making other observations and evaluations of the child.

At the meeting to plan assessment procedures, the assessment team adds their questions to the parents' list. The plan for assessment can then be organized, assigning each question to the most appropriate professionals. The data sources are selected and the locations where the information can best be gathered are indicated. An example of an assessment plan based on possible diagnostic questions is provided in table 3.

Table 3.
Sample assessment plan based on diagnostic questions

Diagnostic question	Personnel	Data source	Location
Is Paul retarded?	psychologist	standardized tests	school
		observation	school and home
At what level is Paul's expressive language?	speech/ language pathologist	standardized tests	school
		language sample	tape at home and school
		classroom observation	school
Does Paul have a hearing problem?	audiologist	pure tone and impedance tests	clinic
How does Paul get along with other children? How often is he aggressive?	teacher	systematic observation	school
		parents	interview at home

The diagnostic questions reflect the parents' and professionals' hypotheses about the child. For example, the parents may feel that their child is retarded and that this is the reason he has so much difficulty at home and in school. If the psychologist determines that Paul is of average ability, then alternative hypotheses must be developed. Perhaps Paul's emotional difficulties are impeding his success. Further assessments are selected to test new hypotheses, using the information from the preceding assessments.

Conduct assessment. Each professional chooses from a variety of formal and informal tests and observation procedures to seek answers to the diagnostic questions. All measures augment and validate the others. Some diagnostic questions can best be answered by a standardized instrument and others can only be answered by systematic observation in a natural setting. When children refuse to be tested, are reluctant to participate, or clearly are not performing as well as they can, more accurate information might be gathered by observation. Three basic types of instruments and procedures for assessing young children are described here.

Norm-referenced tests. Standardized or norm-referenced tests describe how a child's performance compares with the performance of other children who are the same chronological age. Some norm-referenced tests are designed to give in-depth information in one area of development such as language. Many norm-referenced tests have a limited number of items; these items are not necessarily in a developmental sequence. Thus the test only confirms that the child is functioning below others who are the same age. See Appendix A for a list of norm-referenced lists.

Criterion-referenced tests. Unlike the norm-referenced tests, the criterion-referenced test does not measure the child's performance against another's but determines whether or not the child has reached specified levels of competence and development. It attempts to assess very specific skill areas individually; the skill areas are arranged on the test in a developmental sequence. When a child's achievement on the developmental sequence is determined, the teacher can plan instruction at succeeding levels. Criterion-referenced tests are frequently arranged in checklist format and may be used as progress evaluation devices. They are tools to assist the teacher in establishing specific educational objectives. Criterion-referenced tests are listed in Appendix B.

Each of these tests evaluates in detail skill areas such as fine motor development, gross motor development, or self-help skills. The more specific the detail the more potential there is for devising educational strategies for the child. An example from the Learning Accomplishment Profile (Sanford 1974), a criterion-referenced test, appears in table 4. For more in-depth discussion of these tests, see Cross and Goin (1977) and Walker and Wiske (1979).

Observation. In addition to gathering information from tests, the teacher can objectively watch and record a child's behavior during activities that take place during the regular day—noting the child's interactions with adults, peers, and materials. The observations will highlight the child's interests, use of language, patterns of adjustment, and learning characteristics. Aspects of the child's behavior including tolerance for frustration, sense of self-confidence, and independence can be observed in the home or school.

Teachers can plan observations to coincide with activities that require

Table 4.
Example of a test item from
the Learning Accomplishment Profile

Fine motor skills		
Behavior	**Developmental age**	**Credit given if**
enjoys finger painting	30-35 mos.	joy and pride
makes mud and sandpies	30-35 mos.	in product
paints strokes, dots, and circular shapes on easel	30-35 mos.	
cuts with scissors	35 mos.	
picks up pins, thread, etc. with eyes separately covered	36-48 mos.	
drives nails and pegs	36-48 mos.	

Reprinted with the permission of A. Sanford.

a particular ability. For example, to obtain information about the diagnostic question "At what level is Paul's fine motor development?" a craft activity requiring drawing, pasting, and cutting will elicit appropriate evidence of Paul's skills. The teacher develops an assessment map that matches the diagnostic questions with the activities of the day (see table 5).

A thorough discussion of informal assessment can be found in Gunnoe's "Informal Assessment and Individualized Educational Planning" (Meisels 1979b).

Team evaluation meeting. The team evaluation meeting is designed to bring together the results of all the assessments that have been completed. In presenting assessment information professionals should avoid using technical terms or jargon that is difficult for those who are not specialists in the field to understand. Written copies of the assessment should be provided for the parents as well as other team members. These major needs are translated into the goals and objectives of the IEP. After the findings of each participant are presented, the team, including the parents, attempts to reach consensus on a profile of the child's major needs.

Writing the IEP. Where do professionals start in determining goals for the child? The team evaluation meeting yields information and

Table 5.
Sample assessment map

Diagnostic question	Time/activity	Type and frequency of observation
At what level is Paul's fine motor development?	activity time: craft	describe cutting, pasting, drawing during entire activity
How does he get along with others?	free play	record typical sample interactions twice each day for a week
How often is he aggressive?	free play	count number of times he hits or kicks for five days
What is Paul's level of expressive language?	circle	record representative answers to specific questions and spontaneous contributions for three days

recommendations about the child's development, behaviors, and skills that may be improved. The needs identified by the team are grouped into some general focus areas, and parent and teacher priorities are established. The general focus areas used by the EEC include personal/social, gross motor, fine motor/perceptual, and cognitive/language. For each of these areas the EEC has developed a set of goals for all children (table 6); the goals are general enough to include a wide range of functioning and at the same time detailed enough to cover most areas addressed in early childhood programs.

Teachers can devise the long-term goals and short-term objectives (specific behaviors) by adapting these general goals. To individualize the goals for a particular child, the assessment information presented by the team is meshed with the goals for all children in the program. The teacher selects from the list those goals pertinent to the child and adds specific information based on the current level of functioning as determined by the team evaluation process. The following example shows how the Goals for Children can be meshed with the assessment information to produce goals and objectives.

In the team evaluation meeting the participants agree that four-year-old Scott needs to improve his self-help skills as he is approximately two years behind age expectancy. The general goal might be to increase self-help skills. The short-term objectives (eating, toileting, and dressing) are selected from the personal/social area of the Goals for

Table 6.
Early Education Center Goals for Children

Personal/social
1. Develop the ability to express one's feelings in positive and negative situations.
2. Accomplish successful separation.
3. Develop a sense of independence and self-confidence.
4. Increase impulse control and ability to accept limits.
5. Increase the level of attention and involvement in activities.
6. Improve the ability to make transitions and follow classroom routine.
7. Develop ability to make self-regulated choices and complete activities.
8. Develop the ability to eat independently.
9. Develop the ability to be generally independent in toileting.
10. Develop the ability to dress oneself.
11. Develop a positive self-image.
12. Develop trust relationships with teachers.
13. Increase the ability to make friends.
14. Increase positive interactions with peers.
15. Acquire skills of group participation.

Gross motor
1. Develop the ability to run, jump, hop, skip, balance, and climb.
2. Improve body awareness.
3. Increase coordination and agility.

Fine motor/perceptual
1. Increase the ability to work with manipulative materials, e.g., puzzles and art activities.
2. Develop the ability to discriminate among shapes and figures.
3. Develop the ability to cut with scissors and to use drawing implements.
4. Develop the ability to button, zip, tie, and dress oneself.

Cognitive/language
1. Increase the ability to attend to tasks and play.
2. Increase sensory awareness.
3. Increase exploration and mastery of a broad repertoire of curriculum.
4. Increase the ability to differentiate between reality and fantasy.
5. Begin to acquire basic information, e.g., colors, number concepts, and written communication.
6. Develop the ability to match, classify, and seriate.
7. Develop the ability to understand and follow directions.
8. Develop sequencing and memory skills.
9. Improve clarity of speech (articulation).
10. Develop the ability to recognize and name common objects.
11. Learn to use pronouns and prepositions.
12. Develop proper syntax and sentence construction.
13. Develop the ability to communicate effectively.

Adapted from Meisels (1979b)

Children (numbers 8, 9, and 10). Specific information is added to those goals to include Scott's current ability on each as well as additional components that need to be accomplished. The final objectives are then stated.

Scott will: develop the ability to eat with a spoon and cup independently, spilling little;

develop the ability to put on his coat, shirt, pants, and socks independently;

develop the ability to initiate going to the toilet by himself.

On the IEP the assessment information, general goals, teaching strategies, and evaluation procedures are summarized. For the general goal for Scott to increase self-help skills, the IEP could be developed as in table 7.

Table 7.
Sample IEP for one goal

Current performance level	General student-centered goals	Teaching approach and methodology, monitoring and evaluating techniques, specialized equipment and materials
Scott can finger feed	to increase self-help skills	home teaching for feeding, dressing, and toilet training
able to take off clothes independently		individual school instruction for feeding, dressing, and toilet training
wears diapers		evaluation of home and school feeding and dressing
		frequency chart for toileting
		no specialized equipment

The specific short-term objectives to increase Scott's self-help skills would be listed on the next page of the IEP. The IEP also contains:
- a profile of the child;
- details of special education services, complete with personnel, location, frequency, and duration of services;

- criteria for the child's movement to the next less restrictive program;
- name of liaison person who will coordinate the child's program; and
- transportation plan.

The parents must sign the plan and accept the services, goals, and objectives before services begin. P.L. 94-142 gives parents legal rights and procedures to participate in developing the IEP and to challenge the IEP that is developed if they disagree. The steps to resolve any conflicts, which are stipulated in P.L. 94-142 and state legislation, might include additional independent assessments of the child, negotiation with the school, hearings before a judge or administrative agency, etc. Professionals should be thoroughly familiar with the specific procedures governing their state.

Keeping records on the IEP. It is important to document the changes and improvements the child makes on each of the objectives in the IEP. Formal evaluation takes place once a year, but progress on objectives is reported quarterly.

Record-keeping methods should not be too time consuming. As soon as the IEP is written and approved, the teacher determines for each objective the appropriate data collection method to record progress. Data collection methods include frequency recording (how often a behavior occurs), duration recording (how long a behavior lasts), and anecdotal recording (written description of the incident), among others.

The teacher can make a notebook or section of a notebook for each child's objectives with space to record progress. If the objectives are typed with blank spaces for recording the week's progress, new pages for the notebook can be copied easily. The teacher sets aside time each week to record data in the notebook. Table 8 gives an example of how a part of Scott's section might look when completed.

As short-term objectives are accomplished, other objectives further along the developmental continuum can be added. Parents receive written quarterly reports of their child's progress.

Annual review. Once a year the child's progress is reviewed formally. New assessments are completed if necessary to measure growth. The parents and professionals determine at the time of the annual review any changes in the goals, or service delivery for the coming year. As part of the evaluation, the team is required to determine whether the child still needs special education. A new IEP is written after this meeting for children requiring continued special education services. New assessments must be completed every three years for all children involved.

Table 8.
Sample record-keeping method on IEP

Name _Scott_____ Date **week of 11-1**_____

Objective	Data collection method	Frequency	Progress
1. Eat with a spoon and cup independently, spilling little.	anecdotal record	weekly	S. used a cup with a top successfully this week.
2. Put on his coat, shirt, pants, and socks independently.	anecdotal record	weekly	S. can now pull up his pants when requested.
3. Initiate going to the toilet by himself.	frequency record on a chart in the bathroom	daily	Chart: Y= yes N= no

Chart:

	M	T	W	Th	F
1	Y	Y	Y	Y	Y
2	Y	N	N	Y	Y

3 | Setting Up the Classroom

Attention to classroom design and materials selection is crucial in planning to meet the needs of all children in a mainstreamed group (see Kritchevsky, Prescott, and Walling 1977). In describing the setting and equipment used in the EEC, we offer recommendations for all programs based on our experiences. However, each child's disability is unique, so it is impossible for us to prescribe the way in which you might best meet the needs of the children with whom you work.

The EEC is housed in a large, bright, self-contained classroom in a public elementary school (fig. 2). The room contains brightly painted teacher-made dividers and cubbies so that it looks inviting and exciting to children at first glance. The room is organized to appeal to the young child's need for order and organization. Because the program includes children with different types of disabilities, the environment must remain flexible for all children. Generally it is open with wide traffic areas, although specific changes may have to be made when a new disabled child enters, depending on the disability.

We have successfully adapted existing materials rather than purchasing cumbersome and expensive, specially designed materials. For example, rather than purchase a large prone board, we cut down the legs on our sand table to make it accessible for a child who could not stand. This approach, besides saving money, also maintains the appearance of a regular nursery class. Adjustable legs on large equipment such as sand tables or easels would also make the activity accessible to all children. We have adapted regular school chairs for some children, with the direction of the physical therapist, and then painted them so they look special rather than different.

The setting is also designed to achieve a balance between areas for structured, teacher-directed activities and open-ended, child-centered activities. Round cubbylike structures, low pegboard dividers, shelves, and a tall folding divider separate the various areas. All these dividers serve a purpose in addition to partitioning the classroom space, and they are all portable. There is much flexibility and carry-over of play from one area to another.

Figure 2.
The EEC classroom

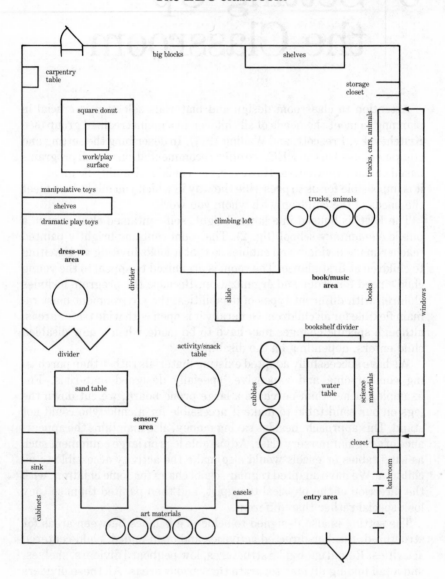

Because the program includes children with different types of disabilities, the environment must remain flexible. Generally it is open with wide traffic areas, although specific changes may have to be made when a new disabled child enters.

As children enter the room, they immediately face their cubbies which are made from large, heavy cardboard tubes, stacked and bolted together. The *entry area* also contains a parent bulletin board for notices, interesting articles and recipes, and a calendar of events, as well as a parent bookshelf.

A *sensory area* lends itself to such activities as water and sand play, cooking, painting, using dough clay, gluing, and cutting. Paper, scissors, and crayons are easily accessible to the children, as is a variety of recycled materials stored in more cardboard tube cubbies. Many teacher-directed activities also take place in this part of the room; there may be three different activities, each at a different table, or there may be one group activity. This area allows for a range of participation, depending on a child's level of functioning. If scissors, glue, paper, and egg cartons are on a table, a low-functioning child might cut paper into small pieces while a more advanced child builds an elaborate sculpture. All the children are still sharing the same media, and the teacher can work with children on the skill areas in which they need help.

A sand table and a water table are considered part of the sensory area. Both stand about waist height for the average four-year-old (about 61 cm). In the sand table are shovels, pails, cars, trucks, dishes, and a variety of containers. The water table has noncorrosive hoses, containers, funnels, boats, and miniature people. Approximately four children can play comfortably around the water table while six can stand around

Children learn to cooperate and share at the sand and water tables.

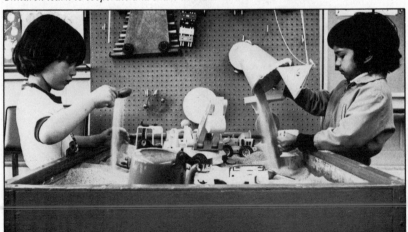

the sand table. These two activities are important parts of the classroom for at least two reasons. First, low-functioning children enjoy spending long periods of time, sometimes all of the 45-minute free play, at these activities. They like to pour and feel the materials, and they are not expected to engage in more advanced imaginative play of which they are not yet capable. It is an effective place to work with them on language skills and concepts, for they enjoy the play, and readily communicate. Second, although sand and water play are particularly suited to children at low developmental levels, higher functioning children enjoy them, too, and often spend long periods of time at them. They sometimes extend their dramatic play into those areas, for instance, bringing a doll to wash in the water table. The fact that all children play at the water and sand tables means that the special needs and regular needs children will be together for some part of free play. They will interact if one wants to ask another for a toy. They learn to cooperate and share, and the teacher can intervene to encourage positive interactions.

A tall divider painted to look like a house with windows cut out of it separates the *dress-up/house area* from the sand play. Hanging from hooks in pegboard are capes, dresses, hats, and shoes. Dolls, dishes, a small table, jewelry, and several other items on shelves can be incorporated into dramatic play. In this area, again, both high- and low-functioning children can find something to use. One might wear a cape while she takes pictures with a toy camera; another might invent an involved game based on the style of hat he is wearing. This section of the room may be seen as a takeoff point for the high-functioning children and an entry into dramatic play for the other children in the group.

Play in the dress-up/house area invariably branches out into the rest of the room. Children build houses and cars with wooden blocks and bring what they need with them. The back of the room, where the blocks are stacked, becomes a bustle of activity during *free play*. Children frequently expand upon ideas from each other's constructions and play. Also in the block area are trucks, cars, people, and rubber animals.

On the other side of the shelves at one end of the dress-up area is a *square donut*. About 12 inches high, this wooden structure is almost 6 feet square, with a 2½-foot square hole in the middle. The children use the donut's surface to work with puzzles, Montessori cylinders, Legos™, stack rings, Cuisenaire™ rods, and other manipulative, concept-development toys. Because of the donut's hole, children can sit opposite each other, or side by side, and they can work together. The donut is also used for teacher-directed small-group activities, such as language development games and stories. When not being used for quieter

When not being used for quieter games, the square donut can be transformed into a house or other dramatic play setting.

games, the donut can be transformed into a house or other dramatic play setting.

The *climbing structure* stands tall in the middle of the room. It contains a loft with a ladder that goes through a trap door to a platform; a slide attaches to one side of the platform. A tire swing, hammock, pulleys, climbing ropes, etc., can be added. The climbing structure provides opportunities for gross motor activity. Some children have to build up courage gradually to climb to the platform, while others have no hesitation.

The *book/music area* serves as the locale for morning circle and other group times. One shelf contains many books which the children either look at themselves or have read to them by a teacher. Another shelf holds the musical instruments, record player, and records.

Because the EEC is incorporated into a large, regular elementary school, the *outdoor playground* is shared with the entire school. It includes three large playing fields and various pieces of standard school playground equipment such as swings, bouncing horses, and hand-over-hand climbers. Many of the pieces are not appropriate for young children because of the scale or the skill the equipment demands. Some equipment was added (a hugh sandbox) and some adapted (rubber backs added to the swings) to make the playground more appropriate. Behind the schoolyard is a conservation area the class visits regularly to experience the changes of flora and fauna throughout the seasons.

The children soon come to feel that the classroom is theirs and they know what is expected of them in each area. Most importantly, each area of the room is equipped with materials that all the children can use in some way. Special needs and regular needs children can play together or in proximity to each other in every part of the classroom. The function of each of these areas is tied to the structure of the day, which is detailed in Chapter 4.

4 | Planning Each Day

Teachers working with groups of mainstreamed children find that it is imperative to plan activities for each day carefully. The staff of the EEC structures the classroom day in an attempt to balance the varying needs of special and regular needs children. Trying to meet all of the specific educational objectives of the special needs children, and the educational objectives for all the children, while at the same time providing a socially active and fun day, is a challenging task. Structured teacher-directed activities which provide specific skill development need to be balanced with open-ended children-directed activities which encourage creativity, independence, and socialization.

Although the children in the EEC program meet five mornings a week, many of the basic principles we outline here can be extended easily for those providing full-day care. Because our program neither provides meal services nor requires afternoon rest periods, we suggest those who are interested seek further information about these two important features of full-day care. References that you may find helpful in planning for food service with mainstreamed groups include *Food for Groups of Young Children Cared for During the Day* (Hille 1960), *Food Service in Child Care Centers* (1981), and *Food, Nutrition, and the Young Child* (Endres and Rockwell 1980).

The morning at the EEC includes time blocks similar to most early childhood programs: morning circle, small group time, free play, snack, story time, outdoor play, singing, and departure time.

To describe the variety of activities that take place in each time block in this chapter we have considered: focus areas, sample skills, teacher approach, sample projects, and a continuum of child participation and teacher support.

There are many focus areas and skills for every activity. For example, cooking incorporates a variety of developmental areas including language, socialization, and fine motor skills. A variety of developmental areas are identified for each activity. Because children's skills will vary in an integrated classroom, a continuum of some possible ways for children to participate in a progression from low- to high-skill development is offered. To define objectives for a particular child, teachers assess the child's entry level on this continuum and make appropriate provisions for increased participation. Children should not be expected to move along the continuum in a linear fashion; nor should it be assumed the continuum represents all the steps in a progression for either child or teacher.

Just as teachers choose the appropriate skill level for a child's participation, they must also determine the appropriate level of teacher intervention to facilitate that participation. Teachers play a crucial role in supporting special needs children's involvement in activities. The EEC plans classroom activities to provide experiences developmentally appropriate for three- and four-year-old children. The special needs children in the program often are not able to participate at that level. Therefore, the teachers must direct and support these children so they can successfully participate at their own levels. The teacher may manually guide a child to begin an activity, offering verbal prompting and direction until the child achieves some success. As the child gains skills and confidence, the teacher support is slowly withdrawn. The child can then participate more independently. While this process may take hours or months, the teacher's purpose is always to support a higher level of participation. The following example illustrates the process.

Joey cannot sit still or participate verbally at circle time. The first level of participation is sitting, which Joey can do when he sits in the teacher's lap. After he learns to sit in her lap without squirming, she gradually diminishes her physical support: for example, Joey sits next to her with her arm on his. While he is learning to sit without any physical support and to pay attention, the teacher encourages Joey's participation at circle time by asking him to perform simple tasks like putting a star under his picture. The teacher physically guides him to do this and gradually eliminates the physical guidance as he gains independence. After he consistently and successfully puts a star under his picture, the teacher begins to engage him in conversation requiring simple verbal responses. At each new step the teacher provides support while Joey learns the skill, fading the support away as he masters the task.

Just as the numerous activity periods of the day require teacher support, so do the many transition times between activities. Special needs children tend to need more help getting from one activity to the next, or in completing tasks such as cleanup or dressing. The children learn these routines more easily if the schedule and structure are predictable. The EEC staff stresses transition times as ways for special needs children to acquire independence as well as to learn to keep up with the movement of the regular needs children. Some teacher interventions used by the EEC staff to accomplish transitions between activities for special needs children are:

Contingency scheduling: Less desirable activities are followed by more desirable activities (cleanup is followed by snack time).

Trying to meet all of the specific educational objectives of the special needs children and the educational objectives for all the children, while at the same time providing a socially active and fun day, is a challenging task.

Manual guidance: Some children need a teacher to hold their hand as they move to another activity to prevent running around the room.

Verbal cues: Just before a transition a teacher gives a child notice about what will happen next. "Jamie, it's time to go outside. Please get your coat." This cue could be reversed by asking, "What comes next?" and having Jamie verbalize what she should do.

Kitchen timer: If a child moves particularly slowly from one activity to the next, stopping frequently at minor distractions, the teacher sets up a "beat the clock" system in which the child is required to get to the next place before a kitchen timer rings. Children are praised or otherwise rewarded for reaching the activity in a reasonable time.

The EEC program places particular emphasis throughout the day on the development of language skills in children. Verbal language is viewed not only as a means of communication but as a system which facilitates cognitive growth. The teachers encourage children to name and describe what is happening by a variety of teaching strategies as demonstrated in these examples.

Modeling: The teacher is sitting with two other children, all working with dough clay. She notes, "My green play dough is very soft and mushy, so it rolls easily on the table."

Questioning: "What color is your shirt, Meagan?" "Can you tell me what you liked about our trip to the farm?"

Expanding: Adam says "Ball." The teacher says, "Yes, you have a big rubber ball."

Expectations: During snack time each child is expected to request the food verbally at her or his highest level. One child might be expected to say "pizza" while another would say "Please pass the pizza, Sheila" before the food is passed.

Humor: Children delight in occasional surprises. The teacher may describe something and intentionally change a crucial element. The children will respond by laughing and correcting the teacher. For example, in warm weather the teacher says, "I see that all of you are wearing your snowpants today." The children laugh and say, "No, we're wearing shorts!"

Listening: Teachers make a special effort to patiently listen to and encourage any and all statements the children make.

As with many developmental areas, speech and language should be encouraged throughout the day and not limited to one activity time. Nonetheless, specific activities in language can enhance and extend particular receptive and expressive skills.

Morning circle   9:00–9:15

Focus areas	Sample skills
communication	talking
attention	listening
socialization	sitting
	following directions
	sharing
	taking turns

Description

As the children arrive in the morning, they gather in a circle on the floor. Two days a week are showing days, when anyone who has some-

Figure 3.

Morning circle: continuum of child participation and teacher support

Level of child participation

Low

sits for portion of circle time	takes turn, sits for duration

puts star up, has turn, and leaves circle
points to children in class when their name is called
shows toy, answers all questions
shows toy, talks spontaneously about it
relates an incident or story in detail without prompt from listeners

shows toy, answers yes/no questions
asks questions of other children
makes spontaneous announcement, answers questions about it

High

Level of teacher support

High

holds child in lap
prompts child for turn
sits next to child with physical contact
asks questions of child that teacher knows child can answer
encourages children to ask questions of each other
helps direct children's attention to speaker
helps clarify questions
encourages children to ask questions of speaker
listens

Low

thing can show it and talk about it. Children and teachers each can have a turn to make announcements every day. This is also a time when daily routines take place, such as putting a star under one's picture to indicate attendance and crossing off the date on the calendar. During circle time, teachers introduce new materials and talk about plans for the rest of the day, such as choices available or special happenings.

Teacher approach

When the children first attend the class, the teachers structure the circle more. They might talk more, ask specific questions of the children, and help them verbally contribute to the larger group (see fig. 3). As the children become more sure of themselves and comfortable with each other, they participate more readily on their own and do not need as much teacher direction. Teachers make sure that everyone who wants a turn to talk gets the chance. They help the children listen and respond to each other by following up on the children's questions posed to other children.

In order to meet objectives for special needs children, some of whom have severe language delays and may be nonverbal, the teacher structures the circle so that these children can also participate, for example, creating some routines requiring physical action rather than talking. While the circle becomes less structured for the verbal children, some consistency is retained as needed for the other children. Although many of the routines are designed to include the special needs children specifically, they are enjoyed by all the children.

Sample activities

Announcements: Children tell about an event, share a toy, ask questions. For children with limited language the teacher might ask a direct question such as, "What are you wearing today, Sandy?"

Calendar: One child puts an X through the day on the calendar. The teacher can help the children count such things as the number of days until a trip or in the week.

Picture matching: Pictures of all the children and adults are taped to a magnetic surface. Each person puts a magnetic star under her or his picture. Children with limited language may be encouraged to say their names as well as those of the other people in class.

Small group time   9:15–9:45

All of the activities available during this time are teacher-directed.

As children become more sure of themselves and comfortable with each other, they participate more readily in morning circle on their own and do not need as much teacher direction.

On some days the choices are announced by the teachers and the children select the activity they wish. On other days children are assigned to work with specific teachers. Activities during small group time are often planned to meet specific objectives of a child's IEP. These have been determined at weekly teacher planning meetings when children, teachers, objectives, and activities are matched. The speech and language specialist and the physical therapist use small group time to work on specific skill development for certain children and to model intervention strategies for the other teachers. The organization remains flexible so that some days there are only assigned groups; other days, a combination of assignments and open choices; and still other days, all choices.

One or more of the following could occur during small group time: art projects, cooking projects, language skills groups, manipulative toy use, small groups working with teachers on structured activities, or a teacher working with one child on a specific objective in the child's IEP which can only be completed on a one-to-one basis. Some of these are activities which some children may not choose on their own during free play, such as Montessori cylinders, sewing cards, or puzzles, but which are important for skill and concept development. It is therefore necessary to incorporate a time into the routine of the day when children will be sure to work on these skill areas.

Sample activity: Pass It On

Focus areas

communication
socialization
attention
cognition

Sample skills

developing growing awareness
  of language
giving specific information
  through speaking
using color and spatial
  concepts
understanding usefulness
  of accurate communication

Description. This activity is part of a communication game approach which demonstrates to children in a very practical way the utility of language. Often groups for language games such as this one meet around the square donut where the noise level is lower. The activity involves from three to five children and is directed by the speech and language specialist or a teacher. The children pass messages to each other; by listening carefully the children can carry out the message.

Materials:

An assortment of colored blocks (two each of four basic colors), and two dividers which can stand on their own, are needed. We use pocket charts, but a large piece of cardboard folded in half will also work well.

Directions:

Children sit on the floor in a semicircle with a teacher in the open part of the circle. The two children at each end of the semicircle have identical assortments of blocks hidden by the divider. The child on the teacher's right places one block on another and whispers a description of this maneuver to the next child, such as, "Red block on green block." Child #2 whispers the secret message to child #3 and so on until the last child receives the message and stacks the blocks accordingly. The children lift their dividers to see if the secret message has been passed correctly. To make the game more difficult, several messages can be passed consecutively without checking, or more blocks with different shapes can be used.

Teacher approach. Depending on the children in the group, the teacher may choose different levels of involvement. For more skilled children, the teacher may give an example of the task and then provide direction only as needed. The children may make some errors, but will discover these errors themselves during the activity. The teacher may need to intervene more when working with children who have limited language or motor skills (see fig. 4).

Sample activity: cooking

Focus areas	Sample skills
cognition	measuring
sensory awareness	observing changes in form
socialization	smelling, tasting, and feeling
attention	foods
communication	sharing
fine motor development	taking turns
	following directions
	describing color, smell, and
	feel
	cutting, pouring, and mixing

Description. From two to four children sit around a table with a teacher for most cooking activities. The teacher reads the recipe, but the children do as much of the measuring, pouring, mixing, and cleaning up as possible (fig. 5).

Materials:

Apple Crisp

10 large apples	bowl
½ c. water	mixing spoon
2 tsp. cinnamon	apple corer (if available)
½ c. whole wheat flour	knives suited to children's
1½ c. rolled oats or granola	abilities (plastic
¼ c. honey	serrated or table knives
⅔ c. peanut butter	are fine)
4 tbsp. margarine	9″ × 13″ baking pan

Directions:

Peel, core, and slice apples. Depending on the children's skills, you may want to use unpeeled apples or peel them ahead of time. Children may be able to core apples and make slices or chunks. Children arrange apple pieces in baking dish and sprinkle with water and cinnamon. Children measure and mix together flour, oats, sugar, peanut butter, and margarine in a bowl, and spread over apples. Children carry the pan to the oven. Bake at 350°F for about 30 minutes, until apples are tender.

Teacher approach. The teacher reads the recipe to the group using a

Figure 4.
Pass It On: continuum of child participation and teacher support

Level of child participation

Low

| repeats phrase | builds structure with teacher and whispers to next child as directed by teacher | builds structure independently and repeats description | replicates structure without help | builds and describes independently |

High

| describes so child can repeat | decides with child what structure they will build | helps child describe structure | helps child interpret message and build replica | guides children to continue game with minimal teacher support |

High   Low

Level of teacher support

Figure 5.

Cooking apple crisp: continuum of child participation and teacher support

Level of child participation

Low											High
stirs	puts apple slices in pan	pours	washes fruit	sets timer	measures	cuts	peels	uses corer	reads recipe	experiments with recipe, adds new ingredients	

High								Low
holds bowl and child's hand, directs movement	gives child bowl with measured ingredients so child can stir		measures ingredients so child can pour	gives correct measuring cup so child can fill it	guides use of cutting utensils	helps place corer correctly	writes recipe with symbols	reviews recipe so children can verify completion

Level of teacher support

chart with words and pictures. Children participate in each step and are encouraged to help each other. Some children will need guidance to complete a task while others will be very independent. Conversation can include how ingredients smell, taste, feel, look, and how they change as they are used in the recipe.

Children always have many suggestions for foods to make for snacks or meals and food preparation should be encouraged as it is a primary means for many types of learning (Wanamaker, Hearn, and Richarz 1979). Cooking can also be related to other aspects of the children's lives: developing sound nutritional habits, studying various ethnic groups (parents enjoy sharing family recipes), or following up a favorite book such as *Stone Soup* (Brown 1947).

Sample activity: art projects

Focus areas	Sample skills
fine motor development	gluing, pasting, painting,
socialization	drawing, and cutting
attention	sharing, taking turns
cognition	sitting
	following directions
	recognizing shape, color, size

Description. The children work at tables on which materials have been placed for the day's activity(ies). The children are free to select other materials from the recycled items and art supplies.

Roller printing. This two-day project requires both individual and group efforts. The children make the rollers one day and print with them the next.

Materials:

cardboard toilet paper or paper towel rolls
synthetic white liquid glue
bits of yarn, fabric (corduroy is especially good), foam rubber, plastic bubble packing material, etc.

tempera paints
paint trays or pie plates
roll and individual sheets of paper
brushes (optional)

Directions:

On the first day children glue pieces of materials on the cardboard rolls. Some children will need help to do this. After the glue has dried for a day, cover a table with mural paper. Children then roll their rollers in

If a child is struggling with a task, another child may be able to help, or if teachers assist, they ensure that the child does the task and feels successful upon completion.

paint (or brush paint over them), then roll the rollers over paper and see what textures appear. Children usually also want to make individual prints to take home. Some may enjoy using each other's rollers or combining two or more on a single sheet. They may wish to use the printed paper to wrap gifts, as greeting cards, or for other projects.

Collage.

Materials:
  Synthetic white liquid glue or paste
  tape in various colors and widths
  scissors
  paper
  Styrofoam pieces, tissue paper, bottle caps, magazine pictures, egg
    cartons, packing bubbles, strings, stickers, etc.

Directions:
  The teacher can cut lengths of tape for less skilled children to stick to paper. Other children can glue pieces of various materials on paper or other materials to create prints or sculpture.

Teacher approach. Teachers may plan an open-ended activity with more than one step so that children can successfully complete the first step or several steps (fig. 6). They help children who need it and take an interest in and comment on every child's work. For some children, it will be difficult to sit at the table for more than a few moments. Brad, for example, needs a teacher next to him, often with an arm around him, to engage himself meaningfully in any art activity. The teacher has to verbally direct almost all of his actions, "The paste goes on the paper, Brad," or "Now put the cutouts on the paste."

  Other children will lose interest after just a few independent steps. The teacher might encourage such a child to extend her efforts by saying, "Taison, you've pasted four squares. Did you see these circles, too?"

  Regardless of how much teacher direction is given, children should always feel that the process is more important than any resulting product, and that the product is truly theirs, not something created to please the teacher (see Lasky and Mukerji 1980 for further teaching strategies in art).

Figure 6.

Roller printing and collage: continuum of child participation and teacher support

Level of child participation

Low					High
sticks precut tape or sticker to paper	glues object to paper/ roller	glues/tapes several objects to roller/ paper	experiments with printing different colors	cuts own pieces and shapes for gluing	finds other items to glue, makes 3-D design does all steps alone

Level of teacher support

High					Low
holds child, directs hand, praises	holds paper so child can put pieces on	provides child with various objects to glue	praises child for using various media	encourages child to use objects in new ways	organizes craft materials so children can work on their own

Sample activity: manipulative materials

Focus areas	Sample skills
visual-motor perception	understanding spatial
fine motor development	relationships
cognition	fitting pieces in holes
attention	matching and sequencing
	stringing beads
	following directions
	recognizing color, shape,
	size

Description. The children can use this equipment (see table 9 for a list of materials arranged by difficulty) on tables, or the floor, or on the square donut. Most children make their own selection, while some work on a specific task with a teacher.

Teacher approach. Teachers generally make available the simpler toys early in the year, adding more difficult ones as children can successfully use them. Year-round programs will need to offer a variety at all times. Children will select that equipment which is at their own level of performance. If a child is struggling with a task, another child may be able to help, or if teachers assist, they ensure that the child does the task and that the child feels successful upon completion of it. Figure 7 contains a continuum for child participation and teacher support with puzzles.

Free play   9:45–10:30

Free play switches the focus from teacher-directed to child-directed play, although the special needs children particularly need the teacher to support, guide, and develop their play. When first presented with a free-play situation in an unfamiliar environment with unfamiliar peers, the tendency of many young children is to play with objects or not play at all. As they become more familiar with the people and their surroundings, it is expected that their play skills will be directed more outwardly, making contact with other people and things. Eventually the children will engage in cooperative social play. In an integrated class the range of play skills is likely to be broader than in a nonintegrated setting, but the environment must allow for this range and present challenges to children at every level. One child may need help playing with a single toy while another may invent involved, imaginative games from the first week of entry into the program. To measure growth, then, one must

Table 9.
Manipulative materials in approximate order of difficulty

one-piece puzzle with knob
one-piece puzzle
stacking rings
shape-sorting box
noninterlocking puzzles
bristle blocks
Legos™
pegboards
number and letter puzzles
Montessori cylinders
matching games
Lotto
design cards
sewing cards
beads to string
interlocking puzzles
board games

look at each child individually. The teacher must be aware of what play skills the child has initially, help the child progress at a suitable rate, and evaluate the rate accordingly.

Children learn through play and through interactions with their peers and environment. School provides an environment where children can explore and learn how things work. Children are developing an understanding of things we continue to learn about for years, including self-concept, human relationships, communication, independence, and group dynamics. During school experience they continue to develop their personalities, explore their individual capacities, become self-sufficient, and learn to relate to other people. The emphasis of quality early childhood programs therefore is on the social/emotional development of the child.

Child-directed play is integral in this development since it allows for interaction and play with a minimum of teacher involvement. The children are responsible for trying to handle their interactions and whatever problems ensue, but the teacher intervenes when they need help. Teachers can help children discuss a problem, lead them to a possible resolution, and model appropriate responses, but distinction should be made between intervening and taking over. Teachers should let children do as much as they are capable of in any situation, knowing that the

Figure 7.

Puzzles: continuum of child participation and teacher support

Level of child participation

Low						High
takes one piece with knob out of puzzle	completes several one-piece or noninterlocking puzzles	completes three-piece noninterlocking puzzles of shapes of various sizes	completes simple interlocking puzzle with 5 or 6 pieces	completes more difficult interlocking puzzles	completes various puzzles with little assistance	does jigsaw puzzle with interlocking pieces

High						Low
manually guides child to put puzzle piece on table and back into puzzle	recognizes that teacher's presence and encouragement are needed to keep child on task	verbally prompts child to put pieces in order	helps child to approach task—suggests looking at design before dumping pieces out	completes more difficult interlocking puzzles	praises for completion and ability to work alone	helps child sort pieces of large jigsaw puzzle

Level of teacher support

In dramatic play children are learning to resolve their conflicts verbally, cooperate with others, and become self-reliant individuals; the teacher's role is to help them achieve these ends.

teacher's role is to support growth. While children are learning that teachers are part of the supportive environment, teachers may take a more active role in free play, getting to know the children and vice versa. As the children progress, teachers observe more but are still always aware of what is happening and where they are needed.

Free play is a good time for teachers to work with special needs children who have low-level play skills and to play with the child to create a successful play experience. If another child wishes to enter the game, the teacher can support the play so that both children have a positive and enjoyable experience. Later, the children often choose to set up this familiar game on their own to repeat their success.

Four of the key activities in free play are discussed in greater detail: sand table, woodworking, block building, and dramatic play.

Sample activity: sand table

Focus areas	Sample skills
fine motor development	pouring, digging
socialization	building
cognition	sharing, taking turns,
language	interactive dramatic play

continued

Sample skills continued
understanding cause and
effect, concepts of full/
empty, conservation
describing, requesting,
questioning

Description. The sand table is described in Chapter 3 (p. 32).

Teacher approach. Children with severe developmental delays often
spend much of the free-play time at the sand or water table. Running
their hands through the sand and digging it with a shovel is gratifying.
Teachers can use this opportunity to play with these children, inventing
games that amuse them while requiring language production. If you
make a game of pouring sand into a bucket, the child might be required
to say "pour" each time she or he wants the action repeated. Other
children at the table might become involved, too, joining in the game
and perhaps modeling the teachers' techniques with the special needs
child. They can then be praised for finding ways to involve their
classmates. Sometimes teachers can enhance the experience of the
children; at other times teachers will observe the sand play and allow
the child freedom to enjoy the activity alone (fig. 8).

Sample activity: woodworking

Focus areas	Sample skills
fine motor development	hammering, drilling
gross motor development	aligning pieces of wood
creativity	gluing
	designing a project

Description. Two or three children can work at a time at our carpentry table, which is always closely supervised. Others work on the floor.
There is a box of scrap soft wood, nails, adult-sized hammers, and a
hand drill with assorted bits. Other tools and supplies could add a great
deal more flexibility and opportunity for children to more fully develop
carpentry skills (see Blau et al. 1977).

Teacher approach. Many children will eagerly build constructions
with which they are very happy. They range from simple two-piece
constructions to ones of more elaborate design. Initially, teachers will
need to model use of tools for children to whom the materials are new.
They may need to help some children manually; for others, observation
and encouragement will suffice (see fig. 9). Children with less motor

Figure 8.
Sand table: continuum of child participation and teacher support

Level of child participation

Low ——— High

| moves hands through sand | pours sand in table | stays at table for period of time, uses variety of objects | interacts with other child in repetitive game | explores materials with little encouragement | builds with dry/wet sand, incorporates toys into play | plays at table with various children and objects for period of time |

Level of teacher support

High ——— Low

| encourages child to participate through teacher's presence at table | helps child to play at table by introducing new objects and ways to play | plays game with toys and involves other children | fades participation while children maintain game | encourages children to use new toys or use toys differently | observes children interacting at sand play |

Figure 9.

Woodworking: continuum of child participation and teacher support

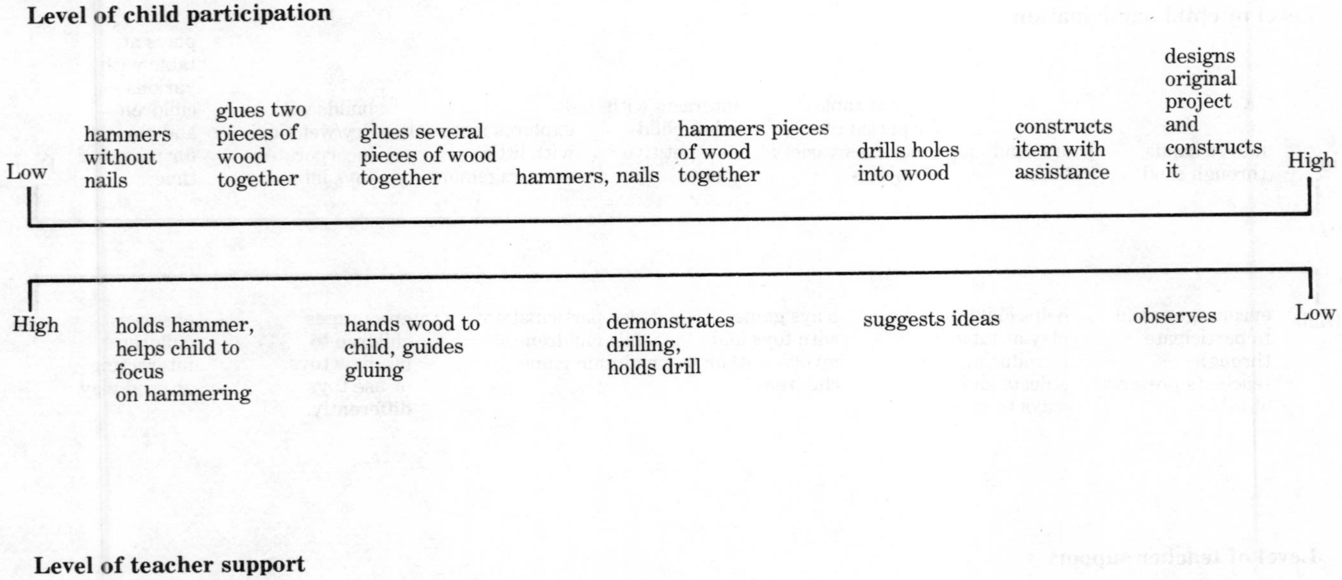

Level of child participation

Low						High
hammers without nails	glues two pieces of wood together	glues several pieces of wood together	hammers pieces of wood together hammers, nails	drills holes into wood	constructs item with assistance	designs original project and constructs it

High						Low
holds hammer, helps child to focus on hammering	hands wood to child, guides gluing		demonstrates drilling, holds drill	suggests ideas		observes

Level of teacher support

control can begin making wood constructions with glue instead of nails. When they seem ready they can be introduced to hammering and other more sophisticated skills. The children may want to paint their constructions.

Sample activity: block building

Focus areas	Sample skills
fine motor development	building with small blocks
gross motor development	building with large blocks
cognition	sorting by shape, size
socialization	comparison
	counting
	understanding cause and effect
	building with others,
	interacting in dramatic play
	describing, requesting,
	questioning
	grasping spatial relationships

Description. Several kinds of blocks are available in the classroom: (1) large, hollow wooden blocks; (2) wooden unit blocks in a variety of shapes, e.g., squares, rectangles, triangles, arches, cylinders; (3) colored plastic cubes and rectangles which lock together; and (4) cardboard brick blocks. The shelves which house the small blocks have two-dimensional pictures of each block shape indicating where they are to be stored on the shelf. The space designated for block play is large enough for several children to be involved in the construction. The hollow blocks are arranged against a wall. Nearby are cars, trucks, people and animal figures, and an airplane, all of which are frequently used accessories with blocks.

Teacher approach. As in all other activities, teachers determine their level of intervention based on the needs of individual children (fig. 10). If the children are not using the blocks, the teacher's presence in the block area may stimulate interest. Another way to create attention to blocks is to use two or three pieces to begin a construction. If children's use of the materials seem to have reached a plateau, teachers' suggestions, questions, or posing of problems may stimulate more involved play (see Hirsch 1974 for details on block building).

Less developed children may start by handling the blocks or knocking over a pile. As they feel more comfortable, the teacher can build with the child. Accompanying verbal encouragement and direction will give

Figure 10.

Block play: continuum of child participation and teacher support

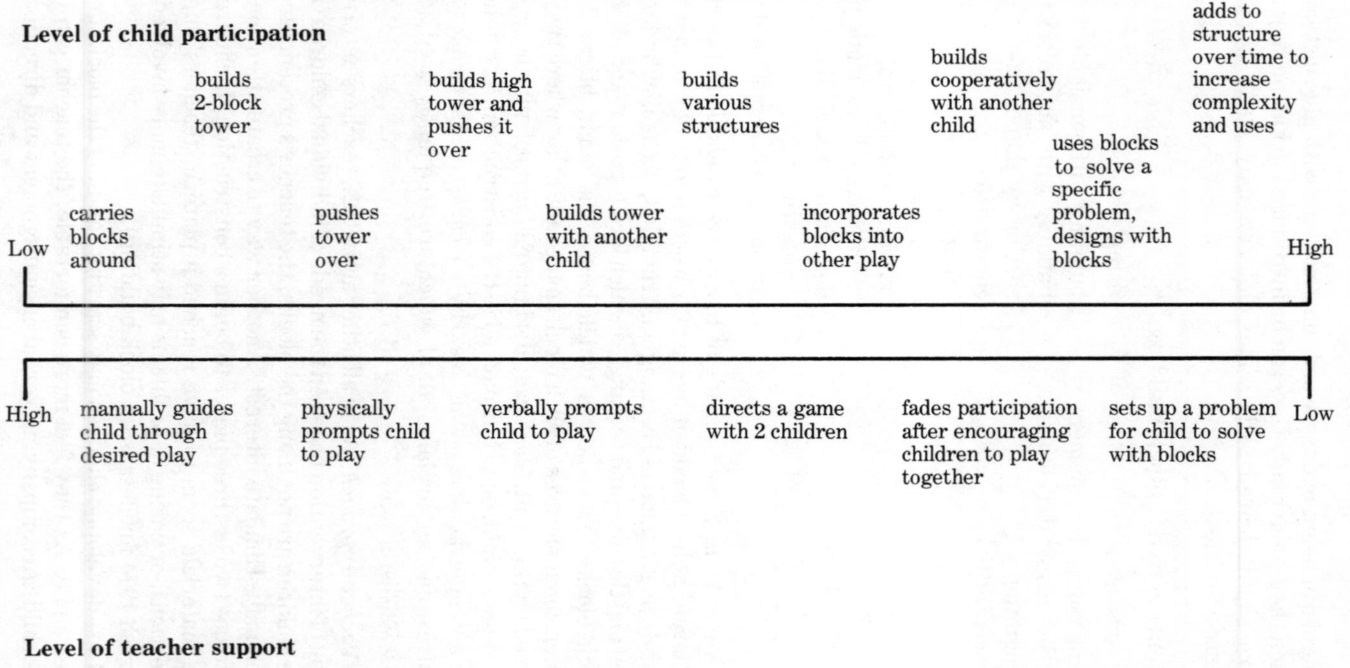

Level of child participation

Low

- carries blocks around
- builds 2-block tower
- builds high tower and pushes it over
- pushes tower over
- builds tower with another child
- builds various structures
- incorporates blocks into other play
- builds cooperatively with another child
- uses blocks to solve a specific problem, designs with blocks
- adds to structure over time to increase complexity and uses

High

High

- manually guides child through desired play
- physically prompts child to play
- verbally prompts child to play
- directs a game with 2 children
- fades participation after encouraging children to play together
- sets up a problem for child to solve with blocks

Low

Level of teacher support

the child labels for materials and help in understanding concepts. The children will also start to see themselves in relation to other things and people as they build tall towers and compare the size to their own heights. This observation is reinforced by the teacher who comments on the children's work, "That tower is taller than you!" "It's taller than me, too." Children can reconstruct their experience in words when the teacher asks, "How did you reach so high?"

The open-endedness of blocks should be accepted by the teachers, as in all activities where there is no right way to approach them. Through experimentation children will discover what methods of stacking blocks are successful and what methods fail. They will probably devise explanations for these problems. The teacher can ask the children about their ideas and help clarify them.

Cleanup is a learning experience as the children sort blocks by shape and size, match them to corresponding pictures, and stack them so they do not fall.

Sample activity: dramatic play

Focus areas	Sample skills
socialization	pretending with an object
creativity	taking roles
language	sharing, leading, following
	using imagination to create
	stories, situations
	talking in imaginative roles,
	describing, requesting

Description. The dress-up area in the EEC is defined by a tall folding divider with windows, shelves holding materials such as telephones and jewelry, and a low pegboard divider. One side of the folding divider is painted to look like a house exterior; the other side is an interior, with hooks on which to hang pots and pans. There is a low round table in the area, with two low, cushioned stools beside it. A pegboard on the wall holds numerous hats, dress-up clothes, and cameras. Other materials include a doctor's kit, dishes, pictures of food, and pocketbooks. Children use these items in all parts of the room in their dramatic play. This enables children to integrate blocks, capes, and cars, for example.

Teacher approach. Teachers might be directly involved in children's dramatic play to introduce possibilities and to help new children feel comfortable with the room and each other. Otherwise, except when intervention is necessary to resolve conflicts, teachers will observe the play, and can note which children can be encouraged to join this type of activity, or which props might be added. As the children increase their cooperative play there will be conflicts: who wants to play which role, who had a certain prop first. If the children have the skills to verbally communicate their wants, then the teacher should allow children to attempt to resolve their own conflicts before intervening. If the child makes no effort to use words, the teacher can ask questions and suggest possible approaches. "How can you tell Jason you want the doll?" For a child with less developed language skills, the teacher can provide the words: "You can say, 'I want the doll.' " "Say 'want doll.' " If the doll is not relinquished, the teacher must help the children work out a compromise. It is important for the children to see that their use of verbal communication is effective. Even if the child who asked is not entitled to the doll, something should be worked out, whether it is a substitute toy or the promise of the doll at a later, specified time.

Children are learning to resolve their conflicts verbally, cooperate with others, become self-reliant individuals. The teacher's role is to help them achieve these ends. By providing diverse, open-ended materials, letting the children develop their own play, and intervening when children need help, the teacher creates a supportive environment in which the children can explore the world and themselves.

Some children are hesitant to dramatize their fantasies. Often just the presence of the teacher in the area will make them feel more comfortable and able to do this. The teacher may be more direct and suggest that one child might enter and play a part in another's game, helping the children accommodate each other. The teacher can take a more active role with the delayed child, inventing simple games when the child puts on a hat or cape. The child may not be able to join in another child's dramatic play to that child's satisfaction, but perhaps she or he will have grown to be less dependent on the teacher and better able to engage in play with the materials at hand.

Children with severe emotional, intellectual, or social developmental delays are not yet able to engage in sophisticated dramatic play. It is not expected that all children in a mainstreamed group will be able to play together. Often there is a child whose imagination is so developed that her or his peers cannot follow the play. Thus, teachers need to ensure a wide variety of play options and levels of involvement for all the children in the group (fig. 11).

Figure 11.
Dramatic play: continuum of child participation and teacher support

Level of child participation

Low ——— High

| plays alone with an object, wears article of dress-up clothing | plays in proximity or peer | plays passive role in other child's play without interaction | develops parallel game with peer object or setting, interacting verbally or nonverbally | engages cooperative play by sharing | takes part in dramatic sequence with specific roles and actions | initiates a dramatic sequence with children |

Level of teacher support

High ——— Low

| imitates child's play to encourage interaction | helps expand game, introduces roles to children | encourages child to develop a self-assigned role | supports interaction between children through teacher involvement in play | provides a variety of props to stimulate the dramatic play |

Snack   10:30–10:45

Focus areas	Sample skills
independence	getting cup
fine motor development	cleaning up
attention	pouring, spreading with a knife
socialization	sitting
nutrition	following directions
	taking turns, sharing
	describing, requesting, conversing, listening
	developing nutritional awareness

Description

When free play is over and the children have cleaned up, they are responsible for going to the bathroom, getting their cups from their cubbies, and finding a place at one of the three snack tables. The food is on the table, and the children help themselves, asking for food to be passed. During snack there is a lot of conversation between children and teachers. The children throw their napkins away and wash their cups when they have finished eating.

Teacher approach

One teacher sits at each table to stimulate conversation, help children respond to each other's requests, urge children to taste new foods, and supervise any food preparation (fig. 12). Children do as much as they can during snack; e.g., if they are having crackers and peanut butter, they spread their own peanut butter. For children just learning to talk, teachers encourage verbal requests. In some cases they ask children to model the appropriate verbal request, "Karen, can you say 'please pass more carrot sticks' so Jamie can hear you?"

Story time   10:45–11:00

Focus areas	Sample skills
attention	sitting, listening
cognition	looking at books, naming pictures, following a sequence, reading
socialization	learning to be in a group
	describing, questioning, answering questions, discussing

Figure 12.
Snack: continuum of child participation and teacher support

Level of child participation

Low					High
sits through snack	repeats requests for food	throws away napkin and washes cup	pours from pitcher	spontaneously asks for food	carries on conversation while eating snack

Level of teacher support

High					Low
sits with arm around child to ensure child will sit at table	models requests for food and praises child when child repeats	manually guides child to throw away napkin and wash cup until child can do it with verbal support	encourages child to make requests of other children to pass snack	helps children to become independent about choosing new foods, serving themselves, and cleaning up	asks children about preparing snack

Description

As the children finish snack they go to the bookshelves, choose books, and sit on the floor to look at them. Some children may choose to listen to a teacher read a story, and in that case one child usually picks the book. The other children read their books alone or with a friend, and there is much sharing of pictures and stories between them (fig. 13).

Teacher approach

A good selection of books for the classroom includes, but is not limited to, some which deal with issues the children face day to day, some which help explain a past or upcoming event (e.g., books about handicaps before entry of disabled child into class), and some which play with language. After reading a story the group might talk about what happened in it. When a story becomes very familiar, the children may retell it themselves. As teachers read books with lines that repeat throughout, they can leave these out and let the children fill them in. One teacher is on hand to respond to children who are looking at books themselves. This group often includes the more delayed special needs children who cannot sit and follow a story being read aloud. They can look through a book and be asked to name what they see in the pictures. The teacher is there to help them do this, either by helping them turn pages, by giving them a word to repeat, or by reading a portion of the story. More skilled children enjoy dramatizing their favorite books and making their own scenery and costumes.

Outdoor play   11:00–11:30

Focus areas	Sample skills
gross motor development	climbing, pumping a swing,
socialization	rolling, jumping, running,
cognition	balancing
	sharing, taking turns
	becoming aware of outdoor life,
	learning to categorize plants
	and animals
	describing, requesting,
	questioning

Description

Swings, sand, monkey bars, a balance beam, and various pieces of climbing apparatus are available in the outdoor playyard. The children

Figure 13.

Story time: continuum of child participation and teacher support

Level of child participation

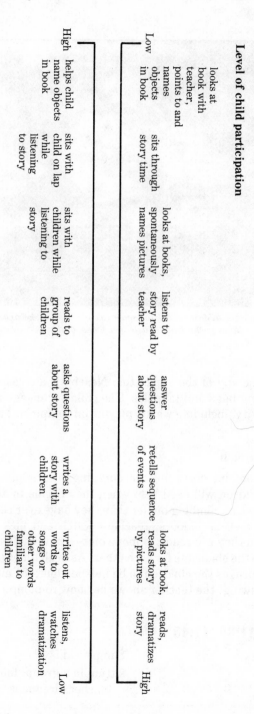

Low				High
looks at book with teacher, points to and names objects in book	looks at books, spontaneously names pictures	listens to story read by teacher	answer questions about story	retells sequence of events
				looks at book, reads, dramatizes story by pictures

High

helps child name objects in book

sits with child on lap while listening to story

reads to group of children

asks questions about story

writes a story with children

writes out words to songs or other words familiar to children

Low

sits with children while listening to story

Low

listens, watches dramatization

High

Level of teacher support

One teacher sits at each table for snack to engage in conversation, help children respond to each other's requests, urge children to taste new foods, and supervise any food preparation.

are free to use any of the apparatus. Nearby is a stream where they enjoy watching bugs and tadpoles. The children engage in all kinds of physical activity, including walks, playing on equipment, and digging in the sand.

Teacher approach

Teachers combine observing, encouraging, and helping outside (fig. 14). Some children will need help when they decide to attempt something new, such as climbing higher than they have ever climbed before. Outdoors as well as indoors, teachers watch and pick up from the children when they are ready to move on to a new challenge. Children often provide the challenge for each other. As in all times of the day, the teacher encourages the children to be independent; if Caitlin asks for a push on the swing, the teacher shows her how to pump.

Singing   11:30–11:45

Focus areas	Sample skills
attention	sitting in a group, following
language	teacher directions

Figure 14.

Outdoor play: continuum of child participation and teacher support

Level of child participation

Low   High

| stays within prescribed physical boundaries | plays in sand | tries equipment with teacher | climbs | finds leaves, insects, etc. | pumps on swings | leads others in play or use of equipment |

Level of teacher support

High   Low

| stays with one child and guides child to equipment | helps child to swing, climb, balance, etc. | helps identify interesting leaves, insects, etc. which children find | follows child lead in playing with others | observes and supports children in being independent outside |

gross motor development   singing songs, memorizing
fine motor development   verses
                                   remembering sequence
                                   playing instruments

Description

The children and teachers sit together in a circle on the floor. One teacher leads the group, usually with a musical instrument, teaching new songs and repeating old favorites. The children are free to request songs, and often a song is sung day after day, so soon they can sing songs with many verses.

Teacher approach

Simple songs and ones that many children already know are good for beginners. The children learn songs best by hearing them often rather than having them broken down line by line (see McDonald 1979). Some songs can be written out with words and pictures so that the children can follow along, guided by the visual cues. Children will participate gradually as they feel more comfortable with singing. Songs with accompanying gestures make it possible for nonverbal children to partici-

Songs with accompanying gestures make it possible for nonverbal children to participate in group singing.

Figure 15.
Singing "The Zoo Song" and "Do Your Ears Hang Low?": continuum of child participation and teacher support

Level of child participation

Low singing							High
sits through singing	performs gestures to song	requests a song	sings	sings and performs gestures	follows picture cues to sing	invents new words to songs	teaches new songs to class
Low							High

Level of teacher support

High				Low
sits with one child, guides child to clap hands	models gestures to song	repeats songs frequently so that children learn all verses	draws pictures and writes words of songs so that children follow visual cues	makes up new songs with children about familiar experiences

pate. Varying a song in speed and/or loudness is an effective way to challenge listening skills and create interest, since children must pay close attention (fig. 15).

Departure procedures are incorporated into singing time which is the final activity of the day. Parents are encouraged to participate daily. They usually arrive in time to sit with their child or a child in their car pool for a few songs. The end of the day is signaled by a particular song, usually "Skip-to-My-Lou." The teacher leading the song will sing a few of the standard verses and then dismiss the children by singing a verse to each child. As a child leaves the circle he might hear "Skip to your cubby, Danny." The child usually finds his cubby, puts on his outerwear with the appropriate adult assistance from either a parent or teacher, gathers his belongings, and leaves. Teachers and parents work together to make the children independent dressers and also responsible for their own artwork, notes to parents, and saying goodbye to classmates.

5 | Parent Education

Under P.L. 94-142 all IEPs written for three- and four-year-olds are required to be developed in conjunction with parents. The type and amount of additional parental involvement and the provision of adult education is dictated by the needs of the child and parents, and the resources available to the program. Parents of young children are usually particularly interested in helping with their child's education. Because parents of these children often spend a great deal of time as the child's caregiver, they are most anxious to learn methods which will improve the child's behavior, communication, or self-help skills. If the special education program can help eliminate a particularly negative behavior (e.g., excessive climbing) or increase a behavior which leads to greater independence (e.g., toilet training), the parents have additional motivation to become involved than they might with more traditional school behaviors, such as reading, which may have less impact on family life.

This chapter reviews various parenting participation used at the EEC, depending on the families' needs. A typical example further describes the kinds of families that might benefit most from a particular service. The selection of any of these methods must also take into consideration parents' schedules, transportation availability, and a host of other factors in which respect for the family is paramount.

Home teaching

In home teaching the teacher or counselor works with the parent and child in the home. This strategy assists the professional in better planning for the needs of the family, and is particularly beneficial for parents who have difficulty coming to school either because of transportation or baby-sitting problems. The focus of home teaching is often to increase the child's skills in daily living activities such as feeding, toileting, dressing, playing, etc. The home teacher can explain the center's procedures or teaching methods to the parent and then cooperatively try them out with the child. Home teaching can also focus on ways to play with the child to maximize socialization and language and cognitive development. Home teachers often help parents schedule their child's day to provide a variety of activities, routines, and rest periods. When the teacher and parent work together with the child they both experience the successes and failures. This often helps diminish the feeling that many parents have that only the teacher can work well with their child.

The home teacher and the parent decide together which skills or activities the parent will work on in the home. They set up specific objectives and activities to try. The parent often learns data collection methods and graphing to keep track of the child's progress. The data collection not only documents the child's progress, but also provides reinforcement to the parent for continuing the program. When teaching methods are consistent between home and school, children will generally learn more rapidly.

Example: Mr. and Mrs. R. found dinner time with their three-year-old brain-injured child to be extremely difficult. She would not stay in her chair and constantly wandered around and stood up in her seat. The home teacher asked the parents to measure how long Sara was able to sit in her chair as a baseline. Together they then planned an intervention which increased her length of sitting and decreased the standing up time. The parents and the teacher fed her something she liked to eat for lunch. Whenever Sara stood up the food was taken away and the parent said, "Sit at the table, Sara." When she resumed sitting the food was returned and the parent said, "You may eat while you're sitting." While she was sitting the parents used a lot of verbal reinforcement such as, "It's so nice to have Sara sitting with us." As soon as she finished her meal she was allowed to leave the table and play. The parents said, "Now that you have sat at the table you can play." The parents tried to increase her sitting time beyond the time she was actually eating by continued verbal reinforcement. During the week following the home teaching session the parents continued to measure Sara's length of sitting as well as the number of times it was necessary to take the food away. The increases in sitting time were charted.

This type of home program can also be reinforced in school during snack or mealtime. The teachers can use the same strategies, words, and data collection. Problems can be worked out cooperatively between the parents and the teacher. The home program gives the parents some systematic teaching skills which can be generalized to teaching Sara other skills as well as increasing their enjoyment of Sara at mealtime.

Center-based parent instruction

There are many instances where parents would prefer to come to the center for instruction or where the school provides the best teaching setting for the particular needs of the family. If parents feel that a home teacher would be an invasion of their privacy, or if there are too many distractions in the home to make the home teaching session valuable, it may be best to have the parent come to school. Many parents welcome the opportunity to get out of the house and focus their full attention on learning about their child. There are a variety of strategies the parent educator can use in the school setting.

Parent observation and participation in the classroom

The parent watches the teachers working with the children and may wish to become involved in some activities. Before, during, and after the class the teacher explains the procedures being used, so that parents can use the same methods at home or as participants at the center. This strategy is particularly appropriate for the parent who has low expectations of the child and believes the child cannot do anything.

Example: The parent instructor wanted Mr. and Mrs. T. to increase their expectations of John's self-help skills. She invited them to the classroom and pointed out all the things he could do for himself—hang up his coat, throw away his napkin, pour his juice, put on his clothes. By watching the teachers guide John in these activities the parents learned how to help John to be more independent instead of doing everything for him. The parent instructor and Mr. and Mrs. T. met after the class and decided which self-help skill they wanted to work on at home. The parents decided to guide John in hanging up his coat when he returned from school and charted how many times he was able to do so. In the following weeks the parents and the parent instructor picked other self-help skills to work on at home.

Parent-child instruction

Just as in home teaching, there are many times that it is important to demonstrate teaching skills to parents with the child. The parent instructor can work with the child and parent in another part of the center for a short period, focusing on a particular skill.

The EEC has found videotaping parents with their children to be an excellent teaching tool. Parents learn a great deal about their interactions when they can see a videotape of themselves teaching/playing with their child.

Example: Mrs. L. wanted to implement a home language program with her four-year-old son, Jamie, who has limited language. The speech and language specialist met with the parent, and they planned the home program. After some preliminary instruction, the specialist and the parent worked together with Jamie. The specialist demonstrated the procedures and then Mrs. L. repeated them. The specialist offered suggestions about when and how this program could fit into their regular schedule. When Mrs. L. felt confident, she began the program at home while she continued to meet regularly with the specialist and the child in school to modify, improve, and expand the program. As the parent was learning the program the specialist videotaped Mrs. L. and Jamie working together. The tape was excellent feedback to Mrs. L. and also provided a record of Jamie's development.

Parent group workshop

A small group of parents (four to eight) meets with a leader (psychologist, counselor, teacher) for a time-limited workshop (usually eight weeks). The workshop focuses on management skills, and participants design individual programs to work on in their families. Typical programs focus on dressing, mealtime, bedtime, toileting, and bedwetting. The parents support each other in trying out new skills. One of the most important benefits of the group workshop is that participants realize that all parents have difficulties raising their children and not all problems are caused by a child's disability. Frequently these groups contain parents of both special and regular needs children.

Example: Mrs. M.'s four-year-old daughter Jennifer's IEP focused on her speech and language as well as her behavior with peers and adults. At home Jennifer had difficulty getting along with her brother (they fought constantly according to Mrs. M.). Jennifer also wet her bed nightly. In the parent workshop Mrs. M. examined her use of nagging as her primary tool to control the children, and her lack of success with that strategy. After acquiring some skills in using positive reinforcement and grasping the need to help children understand the natural consequences of their behavior, she undertook programs to decrease her daughter's bed-wetting and fighting. In the bed-wetting program she rewarded Jennifer every night that she did not wet her bed by a special activity such as fishing. Jennifer was responsible for changing the sheets on the nights she did wet. For the sibling fighting Mrs. M. chose to focus a change strategy on the time the children watched television. If she heard them fighting over which program to watch or which space to sit in, she shut the television off for a brief time until the fighting ceased. The children soon learned that their mother was going to act rather than only threaten to act when they misbehaved. Mrs. M. gained some new and effective tools to manage her children's behavior, and as a result she felt like a better mother because she was not constantly yelling at them.

Individual parent instruction

Some parents feel uncomfortable about group meetings. For example, they might have difficulties with their child that they do not wish to discuss with other people. Parents of children with severe emotional problems often feel hesitant about joining a parents' group or workshop. In these cases the parent instruction may be most helpful if offered on an individual basis. A relationship of support and trust is built as a parent talks with a teacher/counselor (who also works with the child) about the child's problems. The parent may later feel more comfortable about being in a group. Professionals engaging in this process must be especially aware that many of these families may need more intense assistance than center staff can provide. In programs which do not employ trained therapists, staff may want to refer troubled parents to other resources in the community.

Example: Mrs. A.'s child, Paul, had many extreme behaviors. He was constantly moving, spoke in stereotyped phrases, and did not relate well to people. Mrs. A. was embarrassed to take Paul any place and felt very responsible for his inappropriate behaviors. She frequently asked herself, "What did I do wrong to have a child like this?" The focus of the parent instruction was first to help Mrs. A. understand her feelings about Paul. It is important that parents of particularly difficult-to-manage children be given a great deal of personal support. Feelings of guilt and self-blame are often prevalent and nonproductive. Before Mrs. A. could begin implementing teaching strategies with Paul, she and the instructor worked together to achieve some small successes to revive Mrs. A.'s confidence and to strengthen the idea of shared responsibility. For many parents in situations like Mrs. A.'s, the support provided by another person makes it possible for further work with the parent to be successful.

All of these parent education strategies are designed to develop the working partnership between the professionals and the parents to meet the child's and family's needs. If several professionals are working with a family, they need to coordinate their expectations for the home efforts. The parent who is keeping a log of utterances for the speech therapist, and practicing stretching exercises five times a day under the supervision of the physical therapist, and instituting a toileting program in cooperation with the home teacher, may be overburdened.

Attention to the needs of other family members is also crucial. If the special needs child receives an inordinate amount of parent attention the siblings may become resentful of the child and even develop problems of their own. A careful balance must be maintained to include all the family members in the special education of an individual child without overburdening the parents and child and/or alienating the other family members.

Working with mainstreamed groups of children and their parents presents many challenges each day. This book was developed to help those who need basic information about teaching children enrolled in an integrated program and to help parents interact more effectively with their children. Additional sources of information are listed in Appendixes A and B and the Bibliography.

Appendix A
Norm-referenced Tests

Test	Areas assessed			
	Perceptual/ motor	Cognition	Speech/ language	Social/ emotional
Assessment of Children's Language Comprehension. R. Foster, J. Giddan, and J. Stark. Palo Alto, Calif.: Consulting Psychologists Press, 1972.			X	
Auditory Discrimination Test. J. Wepman. Los Angeles: Western Psychological Services, 1973.			X	
Basic Concept Inventory. S. Engelmann. Chicago: Follett, 1967.		X		
Bayley Scales of Infant Development. N. Bayley. Atlanta: Psychological Corporation, 1969.	X	X	X	X
Boehm Test of Basic Concepts. A. E. Boehm. Atlanta: Psychological Corporation, 1971.		X		
Bruininks-Oseretsky Test of Motor Proficiency. R. H. Bruininks. Circle Pines, Minn.: American Guidance Service, 1977.	X			
California Preschool Social Competency Scale. S. Levine, F. F. Elzey, and M. Lewis. Palo Alto, Calif.: Consulting Psychologists Press, 1969.				X
Developmental Test of Visual-Motor Integration. K. Beery and N. Buklenica. Chicago: Follett, 1967.	X			

Norm-referenced Tests continued

Test	Areas assessed			
	Perceptual/ motor	Cognition	Speech/ language	Social/ emotional
Goldman-Fristoe Test of Articulation. R. Goldman and M. Fristoe. Circle Pines, Minn.: American Guidance Service, 1967.			X	
Goldman-Fristoe-Woodcock Test of Auditory Discrimination. R. Goldman, M. Fristoe, and R. Woodcock. Circle Pines, Minn.: American Guidance Service, 1970.			X	
Goodenough-Harris Drawing Test. F. Goodenough and D. Harris. Atlanta: Psychological Corporation, 1963.	X	X		
Illinois Test of Psycholinguistic Ability. S. Kirk, J. McCarthy, and W. Kirk. Urbana: University of Illinois Press, 1968.		X	X	
Kaufman Assessment Battery for Children. A. S. Kaufman and N. L. Kaufman. Circle Pines, Minn.: American Guidance Service, 1983.	X	X		
Leiter International Performance Scale. R. Leiter. Los Angeles: Western Psychological Services, 1948.		X		
McCarthy Scales of Children's Abilities. D. McCarthy. New York: Psychological Corporation, 1970.	X	X	X	
Peabody Picture Vocabulary Test. L. M. Dunn.			X	

Test			
Circle Pines, Minn.: American Guidance Service, 1965.			
Preschool Attainment Record. E. A. Doll. Circle Pines, Minn.: American Guidance Service, 1966.	X	X	X
Preschool Language Scale. I. L. Zimmerman, U. G. Steiner, and R. L. Fratt. Columbus, Ohio: Merrill, 1969.		X	
Sequenced Inventory of Communication Development. D. Hedrick, E. Prather, and A. Tobin. Seattle: University of Washington Press, 1975.		X	X
Stanford-Binet Intelligence Scale-R (4th ed.). R. L. Thorndike, E. P. Hagen, and J. M. Sattler. Chicago: Riverside Publishing, 1986.		X	X
Test for Auditory Comprehension of Language, English/Spanish. E. Carrow. Austin, Tex.: Learning Concepts, 1973.		X	
Test of Language Development. P. Newcomber and D. Hammill. Austin, Tex.: Empiric Press, 1977.		X	
Utah Test of Language Development. M. Meacham, L. Jex, and J. D. Jones. Salt Lake City: Communication Research Association, 1972.		X	
Vineland Social Maturity Scale. E. A. Doll. Circle Pines, Minn.: American Guidance Service, 1965.	X		
Vocabulary Comprehension Scale. T. E. Bangs. Austin, Tex.: Learning Concepts, 1975.		X	

Appendix B
Criterion-referenced Tests

Test	Areas assessed
Assessment by Behavior Rating. E. Sharp. Tucson: University of Arizona, 1975.	All the criterion-referenced tests assess perceptual/motor, cognitive, speech/language, and social/emotional development.
Assessment-Programming Guide for Infants and Pre-Schoolers. W. Umansky. Columbus, Ohio: Developmental Services, 1974.	
Behavioral Development Profile. M. Donahue, J. Montgomery, A. Keiser, V. Roecker, and L. Smith. Marshalltown, Iowa: Marshalltown Project, 1975.	
Brigance Diagnostic Inventory of Early Development. A. Brigance. N. Billerica, Mass.: Curriculum Association, 1978.	
Carolina Developmental Profile. D. L. Lillie. Winston-Salem, N.C.: Kaplan School Supply, 1976.	
Early Intervention Developmental Profile and Developmental Screening of Handicapped Infants: A Manual. D. B. D'Eugenio and S. Rogers. Ann Arbor, Mich.: Early Intervention Project for Handicapped Infants and Young Children, 1975.	
Learning Accomplishment Profile. A. Sanford. Winston-Salem, N.C.: Kaplan School Supply, 1975.	
Lexington Developmental Scale. J. Irwin, C. A. Coleman, et al. Lexington, Ky.: Child Development Centers, 1975.	

Memphis Comprehensive Development Scale. A. P. Quick, T. L. Little, and A. A. Campbell. Belmont, Calif.: Fearon, 1974.

Portage Guide to Early Education, revised edition. S. Bluma, M. Shearer, A. Frohman, and J. Hilliard. Portage, Wis.: Portage Project, 1976.

Vulpé Assessment Battery. S. G. Vulpé. Toronto, Ontario, Canada: National Institute on Mental Retardation, 1969.

Bibliography

Teacher resources

Allen, K. E. "The Language Impaired Child in the Preschool: The Role of the Teacher." *The Directive Teacher* 2 (1980): 6-10.

Allen, K. E. "The Least Restrictive Environment: Implications for Early Childhood Education." *Educational Horizons* 56 (1977): 34-41.

Allen, K. E. *Mainstreaming in Early Childhood Education.* Albany, N.Y.: Delmar, 1980.

Allen, K. E. "Research in Review. Mainstreaming: What Have We Learned?" *Young Children* 35, no. 5 (July 1980): 54-63.

Allen, K.E.; Benning, P. M.; and Drummond, T. W. "Integration of Normal and Handicapped Children in a Behavior Modification Preschool: A Case Study." In *Behavior Analysis and Education,* ed. G. Semb. Lawrence, Kan.: University of Kansas Press, 1972.

Allen, K. E.; Holm, V. A.; and Schiefelbusch, R. L., eds. *Early Intervention — A Team Approach.* Baltimore: University Park Press, 1978.

Apolloni, T.; Cooke, S. S.; and Cooke, T. P. "Establishing a Normal Peer as a Behavioral Model for Developmentally Delayed Toddlers." *Perceptual and Motor Skills* 44 (1977): 231-241.

Apolloni, T., and Cooke, T. P. "Integrated Programming at the Infant, Toddler, and Preschool Levels." In *Early Intervention and the Integration of Handicapped and Nonhandicapped Children,* ed. M. J. Guralnick. Baltimore: University Park Press, 1978.

Apolloni, T., and Cooke, T. P. "Peer Behavior Conceptualized as a Variable Influencing Infant and Toddler Development." *American Journal of Orthopsychiatry* 45 (1975): 4-17.

Ault, R. *Children's Cognitive Development.* New York: Oxford University Press, 1983.

Beeler, A. "Integrating Exceptional Children in Preschool Classrooms." *BAEYC Reports* 15 (1973): 33-41.

Bennet, J. M. "Company Halt!" In *Parents Speak Out: Views from the Other Side of the Two-Way Mirror,* ed. A. P. Turnbull and H. R. Turnbull III. Columbus, Ohio: Merrill, 1978.

Blakley, B.; Blau, R.; Brady, E.; Streibert, C.; Zavitkovsky, A.; and Zavitkovsky, D. *Activities for School-Aged Child Care* (rev. ed.). Washington, D.C.: National Association for the Education of Young Children, 1989.

Braun, S. J., and Lasher, M. G. *Are You Ready to Mainstream?* Columbus, Ohio: Merrill, 1978.

Bricker, D., and Bricker, W. "Infant, Toddler, and Preschool Research and Intervention Project: Report—Year III." *IMRID Behavioral Science Monograph,* No. 23, George Peabody College, Nashville, Tenn.

Brooks, K. W., and Deen, C. "Improving Accessibility of Preschool Facilities for the Handicapped." *Young Children* 36, no. 3 (March 1981): 17-24.

Christophersen, J. "The Special Child in the 'Regular' Preschool: Some Administrative Notes." *Childhood Education* 49 (1972): 138-140.

Clark, E. A. "Teacher Attitudes Toward Integration of Children with Handicaps." *Education and Training of the Mentally Retarded* 11 (1976): 333-335.

Cohen, S. "Integrating Children with Handicaps into Early Childhood Education Programs." *Children Today* 4, no. 1 (Jan.–Feb. 1975): 15-17.

Cohen, S.; Semmes, M.; and Guralnick, M. J. "Public Law 94-142 and the

Education of Preschool Handicapped Children." *Exceptional Children* 45 (1979): 277-279.

Cole, P. *Language Disorders in Preschool Children.* Englewood Cliffs, N.J.: Prentice-Hall, 1982.

Cooke, T. P.; Apolloni, T.; and Cooke, S. A. "Normal Preschool Children as Behavioral Models for Retarded Peers." *Exceptional Children* 43, no. 8 (1977): 531-532.

Croft, D., and Hess, R. *An Activities Handbook for Teachers of Young Children.* Boston: Houghton Mifflin, 1975.

Cross, L., and Goin, K. *Identifying Handicapped Children.* New York: Walker, 1977.

Devoney, C.; Guralnick, M. J.; and Rubin, H. "Integrating Handicapped and Non-Handicapped Preschool Children: Effects on Social Play." *Childhood Education* 50 (1974): 360-364.

Endres, J. B., and Rockwell, R. E. *Food, Nutrition, and the Young Child.* St. Louis: Mosby, 1980.

Food Service in Child Care Centers. Washington, D.C.: U.S. Department of Agriculture, 1981. (FN-64)

Forman, G., and Hill, F. *Constructive Play: Applying Piaget in the Preschool.* Monterey, Calif.: Brooks/Cole, 1980.

Froschl, M.; Colon, L.; Rubin, E.; and Sprung, B. *Including All of Us: An Early Childhood Curriculum About Disability.* Educational Equity Concepts, 440 Park Ave. South, New York, NY 10016; 1985.

Garrett, C., and Stovall, E. M. "A Parent's Views on Integration." *Volta Review* 74 (1972): 338-344.

Granato, S., and Krone, E. *Day Care Serving Children with Special Needs.* Washington, D.C.: U.S. Department of Health, Education and Welfare, Office of Child Development, 1973. Available from: Superintendent of Documents, U.S. Government Printing Office, Washington, DC 20402. Number 1791-0176.

Guralnick, M. J., ed. *Early Intervention and the Integration of Handicapped and Nonhandicapped Children.* Baltimore: University Park Press, 1978.

Guralnick, M. J. "The Value of Integrating Handicapped and Nonhandicapped Preschool Children." *American Journal of Orthopsychiatry* 42 (1976): 236-245.

Hanline, M. F. "Integrating Disabled Children." *Young Children* 40, no. 2 (January 1985): 45–48.

Hayden, A.H.; Smith, R. K.; von Hippel, C. S.; and Baer, S. A. *Mainstreaming Preschoolers: Children with Learning Disabilities.* Washington, D.C.: U.S. Department of Health, Education and Welfare, n.d.

Healy, A.; McAreavey, P.; von Hippel, C. S.; and Jones, S. H. *Mainstreaming Preschoolers: Children with Health Impairments.* Washington, D.C.: U.S. Department of Health, Education and Welfare, n.d.

Hille, H. M. *Food for Groups of Young Children Cared for During the Day.* Washington, D.C.: U.S. Government Printing Office, 1960. (Children's Bureau Publications-386)

Hirsch, E. S., ed. *The Block Book* (rev. ed.). Washington, D.C.: National Association for the Education of Young Children, 1984.

Hohmann, M.; Banet, B.; and Weikart, D. *Young Children in Action.* Ypsilanti, Mich.: High/Scope, 1979.

Kaiser, C. E., and Nadeau, J. B. E. *Young and Special: A Multi-Media Inservice Training Course for the Preparation of Preschool Teachers and Aides in Providing Mainstream Special Services for Children Ages 3–5.* Hanover, N.H.: Dartmouth Medical School, Department of Psychiatry.

Karnes, M. B., and Zehrbach, R. R. *Differential Involvement of Parents in an Educational Program for the Handicapped: Parents Are Human.* Champaign: University of Illinois, Institute for Research in Exceptional Children, #1040, 1976.

Kennedy, P. K.; Northcott, W.; McCawley, R.; and Williams, S. M. "Longitudinal Sociometric and Cross-Sectional Data on Mainstreaming Hearing Impaired Children." *Volta Review* 78 (1976): 71-81.

Kieran, S. S.; Connor, F. P.; von Hippel, C. S.; and Jones, S. H. *Mainstreaming Preschoolers: Children with Orthopedic Handicaps.* Washington, D.C.: U.S. Department of Health, Education and Welfare, n.d.

Klein, J. W. "Mainstreaming the Preschooler." *Young Children* 30, no. 5 (July 1975): 317-326.

Kritchevsky, S.; Prescott, E.; and Walling, L. *Planning Environments for Young Children: Physical Space.* Washington, D.C.: National Association for the Education of Young Children, 1977.

LaPorta, R. A.; McGee, D. I.; Simmons-Martin, A.; Vorce, E.; von Hippel, C. S.; and Donovan, J. *Mainstreaming Preschoolers: Children with Hearing Impairment.* Washington, D.C.: U.S. Department of Health, Education and Welfare, n.d.

Lasky, L., and Mukerji, R. *Art: Basic for Young Children.* Washington, D.C.: National Association for the Education of Young Children, 1980.

Levine, M. H. and McColoum, J. A. "Peer Play and Toys: Key Factors in Mainstreaming Infants." *Young Children* 38, no. 5 (July 1983): 22–26.

Lynch, E. W.; Simmons, B. H.; von Hippel, C. S.; and Shuchat, J. *Mainstreaming Preschoolers: Children with Mental Retardation.* Washington, D.C.: U.S. Department of Health, Education and Welfare, n.d.

McDonald, D. T. *Music in Our Lives: The Early Years.* Washington, D.C.: National Association for the Education of Young Children, 1979.

McLoughlin, J. A., and Kershman, S. M. "Mainstreaming in Early Childhood: Strategies and Resources." *Young Children* 34, no. 4 (May 1979): 54-65.

Meisels, S. J. *Developmental Screening in Early Childhood: A Guide* (3rd ed.). Washington, D.C.: National Association for the Education of Young Children, 1989.

Meisels, S. J. "First Steps in Mainstreaming: Some Questions and Answers." *Young Children* 33, no. 1 (November 1977): 4-13.

Meisels, S. J., ed. *Special Education and Development: Perspectives on Young Children with Special Needs.* Baltimore: University Park Press, 1979.

Morgan, D., and York, M. E. "Ideas for Mainstreaming Young Children." *Young Children* 36, no. 2 (January 1981): 18-25.

Muir, K. A.; Milan, M. A.; Branston-McLean, M. E.; and Berger, M. "Advocacy Training for Parents of Handicapped Children: A Staff Responsibility." *Young Children* 37, no. 2 (January 1982): 41–46.

Northcott, W. H. "Candidate for Integration: A Hearing-Impaired Child in a Regular Nursery School." *Young Children* 25, no. 6 (September 1970): 367-380.

Paul, J. L. *Understanding and Working with Parents of Children with Special Needs.* New York: Holt, Rinehart & Winston, 1981.

Peck, C. A.; Apolloni, T.; Cooke, T. P.; and Cooke, S.R. "Teaching Develop-
mentally Delayed Toddlers and Preschoolers to Imitate the Free-Play Behav-
ior of Nonretarded Classmates: Trained and Generalized Effects." In *Early
Intervention and the Integration of Handicapped and Nonhandicapped
Children*, ed. M. J. Guralnick. Baltimore: University Park Press, 1978.
Peterson, C.; Peterson, J.; and Scriven, G. "Peer Imitation by Nonhandicapped
Preschoolers." *Exceptional Children* 43 (1977): 223-225.
Peterson, N. L., and Haralick, J. G. "Integration of Handicapped and Non-
handicapped Preschoolers: An Analysis of Play Behavior and Social Interac-
tion." *Education and Training of the Mentally Retarded* 12 (1977): 235-245.
Rister, A. "Deaf Children in Mainstream Education." *Volta Review* 77 (1975):
279-290.
Sapon-Shevin, M. "Teaching Children About Differences: Resources for Teach-
ing." *Young Children* 38, no. 2 (January 1983): 24–32.
Simon, C. P., and Gillman, A. E. "Mainstreaming Visually Handicapped Pre-
schoolers." *Exceptional Children* 45 (1979): 463.
Snyder, L.; Cooke, T. P.; and Apolloni, T. "Integrated Settings at the Early
Childhood Level: The Role of Nonretarded Peers." *Exceptional Children* 43
(1977): 262-266.
Strain, P. S., and Timm, M. "An Experimental Analysis of Social Interaction
Between a Behaviorally Disordered Preschool Child and Her Classroom
Peers." *Journal of Applied Behavior Analysis* 7 (1974): 583-590.
Turnbull, H. R., III. "Parents and the Law." In *Understanding and Working
with Parents of Children with Special Needs*, ed. J. L. Paul. New York: Holt,
Rineholt & Winston, 1981.
Walker, D. K., and Wiske, M. S. *A Guide to Developmental Assessments for
Young Children*. Boston: Massachusetts Department of Education, 1979.
Wanamaker, N.; Hearn, K.; and Richarz, S. *More Than Graham Crackers:
Nutrition Education and Food Preparation with Young Children*.
Washington, D.C.: National Association for the Education of Young
Children, 1979.
White, B. P. with Phair, M. A. "'It'll Be a Challenge!' Managing Emotional Stress
in Teaching Disabled Children." *Young Children* 41, no. 2 (January 1986):
44–48.
Wishon, P. M. "Serving Handicapped Young Children: Six Imperatives." *Young
Children* 38, no. 1 (November 1982): 28–32.
Wynne, S.; Brown, J. K.; Dakof, G.; and Ulfelder, L. S. *Mainstreaming and
Early Childhood Education for Handicapped Children: A Guide for
Teachers and Parents*. Washington, D.C.: U.S. Office of Education, Bureau
of Education for the Handicapped, 1975.
Wynne, S.; Ulfelder, L. S.; and Dakof, G. *Mainstreaming and Early Child-
hood Education for Handicapped Children: Review and Implications of
Research*. Washington, D.C.: U.S. Department of Health, Education and
Welfare, 1975.

Children's books

Biklen, D., and Barnes, E. *You Don't Have to Hear to Cook Pancakes*.
Syracuse, N.Y.: Human Policy Press, 1978.
    This is a humorous workbook that encourages children to be more aware
and understanding of special needs and differences among people.

Biklen, D., and Sokoloff, M., eds. *What Do You Do When Your Wheelchair Gets a Flat Tire?* New York: Scholastic, 1978.
The book features questions about disabilities frequently asked by children, with answers provided by a range of disabled peers.

Brightman, A. J., and Storey, K. S. *Hollis Being Me.* New York: Scholastic, 1978.
This book gives insight into the life of a child with cerebral palsy.

Brown, M. *Stone Soup.* New York: Scribner, 1947.
A village is conned into supplying ingredients for some hungry soldiers' soup.

Fassler, J. *Don't Worry Dear.* New York: Behavioral Publications, 1969.
Jenny's mother patiently waits for her to outgrow her thumb sucking, bed-wetting, and stuttering.

Fassler, J. *Howie Helps Himself.* Chicago: Whitman, 1975.
Beautiful artwork and a simple text reveal the struggles and successes of a young child handicapped by cerebral palsy.

Fassler, J. *One Little Girl.* New York: Behavioral Publications, 1969.
While Laurie is slow at doing some things, she is fast at others, and when the grown-ups around her finally realize that fact, Laurie is at last happy to be herself. The book provides an understanding of mental retardation.

Gardner, R. A. *MBD: The Family Book about Minimal Brain Dysfunction.* New York: Jason Aronson, 1973.
The first part of this book is written for parents of children diagnosed as having organic minimal brain dysfunction. The book's second part is for children diagnosed as having MBD. Illustrated with cartoonlike drawings, this part can be read aloud to young children.

Grealish, M. J. V. B., and Grealish, C. A. *Amy Maria,* Syracuse, N.Y.: Human Policy Press, 1975.
Told from the perspective of a disabled child, this story is exciting and reveals the drama about Amy Maria's self-concept.

Grealish, M. J. V. B., and Grealish, C. A. *The Sneely-Mouth Snerds and the Wonder Octopus.* Syracuse, N.Y.: Human Policy Press, 1975.
Exciting pictures and text in this fantasy story are helpful in giving insight into the world of the disabled.

Klein, G. W. *The Blue Rose.* New York: Lawrence Hill, 1974.
Just as the blue rose is different from other roses, so Jenny, a mentally retarded child, is different from other people. The text points out that being different is not necessarily bad; yet sometimes people notice only differences and fail to see the whole person.

Lasker, J. *He's My Brother.* Chicago: Whitman, 1974.
This story of Jamie presents realistic experiences of a child with learning disabilities. It helps the reader understand the feelings of the disabled child as he works and plays among children without learning problems.

Levine, E.S. *Lisa and Her Soundless World.* New York: Behavioral Publications, 1974.
A little girl with impaired hearing learns through various methods to use and understand speech.

Litchfield, A. B. *A Button in Her Ear.* Chicago: Whitman, 1976.
Angela explains how she got a hearing aid and how it helps her. This helps people around Angela to better understand about her hearing loss.

Nadas, P. P. *Danny's Song.* Pittsburgh: Family Communications, 1975.

Though Danny can do many things, he sometimes cannot keep up with his brother and sister. The hurt and anger Danny feels about wearing crutches and braces are well portrayed within the context of a loving family.

Peter, D. *Claire and Emma.* New York: John Day, 1976.

A true story of two girls, ages two and four, who were born deaf. Color photos show them with their hearing aids at home and with special earphones at school as they learn to speak.

Peterson, J. W. *I Have a Sister: My Sister Is Deaf.* New York: Harper & Row, 1977.

The narrator of this story knows her deaf sister is special; she can "feel" when a dog barks and knows what people are thinking by watching their eyes. The two children appreciate each other and share in new discoveries.

Peterson, P. *Sally Can't See.* New York: John Day, 1974.

Sally is 12 years old and was born blind. Children will learn about Braille, a white cane, and other ways to compensate for the loss of one sense.

Sobol, H. *My Brother Steven Is Retarded.* New York: Macmillan, 1977.

This simple story with photos of Beth, age eleven, and her older retarded brother is a sensitive portrayal of Beth's feelings of fear, anger, jealousy, and embarrassment toward her brother.

Stein, S. B. *About Handicaps: An Open Family Book for Parents: Parents and Children Together.* New York: Walker, 1974.

A pictorial account of a child with braces and another child's reaction to him.

Wolf, B. *Anna's Silent World.* Philadelphia: Lippincott, 1977.

Born almost totally deaf, Anna lives in a world of muted sounds. Via this photo essay, the reader sees Anna learning to function normally and sees the people and machines that help her.

Wolf, B. *Don't Feel Sorry for Paul.* Philadelphia: Lippincott, 1974.

Photos and a simple text capture two weeks in the life of a handicapped boy learning to live successfully in a world made for people without handicaps. Paul is a seven-year-old with arm and leg prostheses.

Parent resources

Behavior management

Abidin, R. *Parenting Skills.* Human Sciences Press, Inc., 72 Fifth Ave., New York, NY 10011.

For use in parent workshops on management. Uses elements of a variety of approaches. The leader can choose different lessons to meet the needs of the group.

Dreikurs, R. *The Challenge of Child Training: A Parent Guide.* New York: Hawthorn Books, 1972.

This is an abridged version of Dreikurs's *The Challenge of Parenthood;* it presents a philosophy that is sensitive to the needs of children but places the question of power and setting limits squarely in the hands of the parent.

Faber, A., and Mazlich, E. *Liberated Parents and Liberated Children.* New York: Grossett & Dunlap, 1974.

This sensitive book was written by parents who attended two years of workshops with Haim Ginott. It records their experiences in trying to apply his ideas.

Patterson, G. *Families*. Champaign, Ill.: Research Press, 1971.

Semiprogrammed text designed to teach basic behavioral principles. The book is parent centered and encourages firm limit setting.

Systematic Training for Effective Parenting (STEP). American Guidance Service, P.O. Box 190, Circle Pines, MN 55014.

Workshop kit that includes handbooks, cassettes, posters, and charts. Teaches parents management skills combining a variety of approaches such as natural consequences, behavior modification, and active listening.

Speech and language

Getting Your Baby Ready to Talk: A Home Study Plan for Infant Language Development. Los Angeles: John Tracy Clinic, 1968.

A home program for deaf-blind children.

Learning Language at Home. M. Karnes. Council for Exception Children, 1920 Association Dr., Reston, VA 22091.

Activities on cards that can be sent home. The activities are divided into four areas: learning to listen, look, tell, and do.

Parent-Infant Communication. Dormac, 8034 S.W. Nimbus, Beaverton, OR 97005.

Loose-leaf notebook with curriculum for parents of hearing-impaired children birth to four years old. Teaches parents to establish objectives and details activities.

Other commercially available programs such as the *GOAL* program and the *Small Wonders* program (American Guidance Service 1980) can also be used effectively in home programs.

General parent-child activities

Ault, R. *Kids Are Natural Cooks*. Cambridge, Mass.: Parents Nursery School, 1972.

Written for teachers and parents who want to cook with young children, this book provides a collection of recipes that are fun to make, taste good, and are nutritious.

Barratta-Lorton, M. *Workjobs for Parents*. Reading, Mass.: Addison-Wesley, 1972.

Examples of games that can be made at home from commonly available materials.

Caney, S. *Toybook*. New York: Workman Publishing Co., 1972. *Playbook*. New York: Workman Publishing Co., 1975.

Describe toys and games that can be made easily at home.

Cole, A.; Haas, C.; Bushell, F.; and Weinberger, B. *I Saw a Purple Cow and 100 Other Recipes for Learning*. Boston: Little, Brown, 1972.

Describes rainy day activities: things that can be made from readily available materials.

Gordon, I. J. *Child Learning Through Child Play.* New York: St. Martin's Press, 1972.

Describes basic activities appropriate for two- and three-year-olds.

Jones, S. *Learning for Little Kids.* Boston: Houghton Mifflin, 1979.

Source of activities and ways to deal with issues such as death and illness.

Skelsy, A., and Huckaby, G. *Growing Green.* New York: Workman Publishing Co., 1976.

Especially for teachers, parents, and children who want to garden together indoors and outdoors.

For parents of special needs children

Exceptional Parent Magazine, Psy-Ed Corp., 605 Commonwealth Ave., Boston, MA 02115.

Published six times a year, this magazine contains articles of interest to parents of special needs children. Past issues have dealt with topics such as testing, IEPs, parent-school conferences, and mainstreaming.

Featherstone, H. *A Difference in the Family.* New York: Basic Books, 1980.

Written by a parent of a severely handicapped child, this book describes the psychological experience for a family when there is a child who is different.

Finnie, N. *Handling the Young Cerebral Palsied Child at Home.* New York: Dutton, 1975.

A detailed resource for parents of physically handicapped chldren. Includes such practical topics as feeding, bathing, and positioning, complete with illustrations.

Turnbull, A. P., and Turnbull, H. R. *Parents Speak Out.* Columbus, Ohio: Merrill, 1978.

Each chapter is written by a parent of a special needs child who is also a professional in education or psychology. Contributors present their "views from the other side of the two-way mirror."

Index

Information about
NAEYC

NAEYC is ...

... a membership-supported organization of people committed to fostering the growth and development of children from birth through age eight. Membership is open to all who share a desire to serve and act on behalf of the needs and rights of young children.

NAEYC provides ...

... educational services and resources to adults who work with and for children, including

- **Young Children,** *the* journal for early childhood educators
- **Books, posters, videos, and brochures** to expand professional knowledge and commitment to young children, with topics including infants, curriculum, research, discipline, teacher education, and parent involvement
- An **Annual Conference** that brings people from all over the country to share their expertise and advocate on behalf of children and families
- **Week of the Young Child** celebrations sponsored by NAEYC Affiliate Groups across the nation to call public attention to the needs and rights of children and families
- **Insurance plans** for individuals and programs
- **Public affairs information** for knowledgeable advocacy efforts at all levels of government and through the media
- The **National Academy of Early Childhood Programs,** a voluntary accreditation system for high-quality programs for young children
- The **Information Service,** a centralized source of information-sharing, distribution, and collaboration

For **free** information about membership, publications, or other NAEYC services...
... call NAEYC at 202-232-8777 or 800-424-2460 or write to **NAEYC, 1834 Connecticut Avenue, N.W., Washington, DC 20009-5786**

EP 36